RETIRE BEFORE
COLLEGE

THE SECRETS AND METHODS
OF TEEN ENTREPRENEURS

howdy interactive

Dedication

This book is dedicated to Joe Polish
and Walt Disney, both of whom inspired me
immensely in the world of business.

About the Author

Nathan Sykes is a teen entrepreneur and the founder of Howdy Interactive, the world's leading flat-rate marketing firm that gives companies access to a suite of marketing resources for a low monthly retainer.

Nathan works with small businesses and Fortune 500 companies to grow the amount of marketing-qualified leads they have coming into their business.

He's worked alongside companies like NBC, Amazon, Five Guys, Eventbrite, and hundreds more. He owns and operates Howdy alongside his non-profit organization, the Maine Student Film Festival.

Nathan is also a speaker and consultant for large corporations and academic entities looking to cater to young entrepreneurs.

For media inquiries, please visit our website at **go.Nathan-Sykes.com/bmk**

Important Announcement

This Book Is <u>Interactive!</u>

To get free updates for life, our video masterclass, and to stay updated on *everything* we're doing at Howdy Interactive HQ, join our community below:

go.Nathan-Sykes.com/retire-before-college

You have my word - I'll never spam you, sell your info, or try and actively screw you over in any way. If you have questions, there's a contact email on the page - feel free to get in touch with me!

Table Of Contents

Introduction

The Book

Extras

Introduction

Hello! My name is Nathan - thanks for picking up this book.

I've been fascinated with entrepreneurship since I got my first computer at five years old, and my first bank account at seven.

I knew growing up that the "9-5" job for 40 years wouldn't work for me. There was too much to see and do in the world to warrant spending most of my life behind a desk working for someone else.

At 12 years old, I hired a few kids from China who were good at programming plugins for the popular game Minecraft. My first entrepreneurial venture was charging third parties $18/hr for coding, and then paying $5/hr to the people who were actually doing the work.

I quickly realized that I was doing nothing but telling the developers in China exactly what the client wanted. All I had to do was sit back and wait for my $13/hr to roll in.

The developers in China quickly realized I was getting paid more than double what they were for basically sitting on my ass, and I never heard from them again. But from that moment on, I was completely hooked in the world of entrepreneurship.

Chances are, if you're reading this, you are a student that's interested in entrepreneurship, or you're reading the introduction to see if this would be a perfect gift for someone who you think might be interested in the big world of business.

My advice? Get the book. For yourself or for someone you know who this would be perfect for.

I've spent a lot of time and energy compiling some of the best tips, tricks, resources, and content that you can find on running and scaling a business as a high school or college student. I've also interviewed some of the world's foremost experts on teen entrepreneurship, and some of the most high performing teen entrepreneurs in America.

I'm not into coddling people. This book is the first one like it on the market. When you google "teen entrepreneur books", you get a lot of pretentious bullshit about lemonade stands and girl scout cookies, "saving money in a bank and watching it grow", and other content geared at 11-12 year olds.

This is not that kind of book. I'm going to teach you how to make real money. The cover said you could retire before college, and I fully intend to give you the resources you need to succeed in making the words on the cover of this book true.

This is exactly the same methodology that I use every day to lead my team at Howdy Interactive, and that hundreds of other high-performing teen entrepreneurs use to climb the path to financial freedom.

This book will talk about how to *really* invest your money, how to set yourself up for success from a young age, and how to deal with the limitations of being a high school/college student in the big world of business.

We'll go into heavy detail about your mindset, where your money should be, and how to find a problem to solve. I'll then talk about how to market your company using the same strategies I use for my $53,500+ retainer clients at Howdy Interactive.

In terms of sales, we've invested $75k in sales training programs over the years that have turned every single one of my team members into master closers, no matter what their position at Howdy is. I'll take you through the most important bits you need to know to set yourself up for success.

Howdy Interactive has one of the leading complementary PR services in the world, exclusively available for all of our retainer members. I'll teach you how to pitch reporters, find stories, and use the "teen entrepreneur" angle to your advantage.

Finally, Tony Robbins hired his first employee at age 17, and the world of teen entrepreneurship is no different. I'll walk you through best hiring practices, and ways to run your company that maximize productivity from relatively young talent, like high school and college students.

This is not a book about how to run a school fundraiser that raises $800 for your chess club. This book is proven theory, taken from high-performing teens around the world, who deal with five-figure contracts and six/seven-figure salaries at a remarkably young age.

If you're looking for a book that mentally pushes you to reach your limit, and to truly start your climb to financial freedom, then congratulations. Welcome home.

As mentioned in the first few pages, this book is entirely interactive. Keep an eye out for the **go.Nathan-Sykes.com** links, as they're your key to accessing exclusive resources, getting exclusive content, and in some cases, earning awesome rewards.

If you feel like entrepreneurship is for you, and you feel driven to retire by the time you graduate from college, then there's no time to waste.

Let's get started!

Nathan Sykes

Chapter 1: Money

If you don't have your money right, don't bother starting a business. You'll be going in a circle, and end up right back at the beginning.

"Rich people invest. Poor people spend."
- Grant Cardone

"It's not the employer who pays the wages. Employers only handle the money. It's the customer who pays the wages."
- Henry Ford

"The best thing money can buy is financial freedom."
- Rob Berger

There is no way you will be able to live the life you want to live unless you get a handle on your finances. The earlier you start this practice, the better. Not only will you be able to retire earlier, but you'll have financial discipline as you move through high school and college, and get your first taste at success as a teen entrepreneur.

However, if you immediately go and blow your earnings without giving it a chance to grow, then you're back at square one, with no money to look forward to in the future.

I talk a lot about the concept of "Financial Freedom" in this book. The definition of financial freedom is different for everyone. For the purposes of this book, we're going to assume it's making enough money where you can stop working a day-to-day job (whether that's for someone else or for your own company!), and live comfortably, relying on passive income.

Financial freedom is the gateway to the life you want to strive for. I like to live large, so my number to achieve financial freedom is $50 million dollars. I know some teens that just want to own a farm in Idaho and relax, so their number to achieve financial freedom is much lower. It really depends on what kind of life you want to live, and how hard you're willing to work from a young age to get there.

I mentioned passive income, which is your biggest friend on the climb to financial freedom. Passive income is defined as anything that makes you money that you don't exert consistent physical effort towards. The most common form of passive income are investments, either in the stock market, real estate, or a startup company. However, passive income can take the shape of book royalties, licensing agreements, and even monthly subscription access to your products.

In fact, that's what we do at my marketing firm, Howdy Interactive! We charge our clients on a monthly retainer model, so they pay us every month instead of per-project. Our business model has about a 20% profit margin, so we know that we'll make about $10,000/yr in profit per client, just by providing our services. Since I'm not directly involved in day-to-day operations anymore, this is a viable form of passive income for me.

The truth is, there are a plethora of tools that you can use to your advantage to grow your wealth, theoretically from the time you're in high school.

Investing your money should be a no-brainer, but there are plenty of other awesome resources that you can use to maximize your cash flow, leverage debt (the good kind!), and earn more income.

The bad news is that the vast majority of these tools may not be available to you initially. You may still be a minor, which means you can only open bank accounts with a parent or guardian present. Your credit score may be too low to qualify for any life-changing credit cards or loans. We'll talk about all sorts of ways you can start to use these tools to climb to financial freedom, so you're better prepared to use them when the time comes.

The good news is that you're off to a head start! The vast majority of students don't even think to start the conversation about their financial wellbeing until it's too late. They're drowning in debt, opening crappy credit cards left and right, and racking up bills faster than the shitty, minimum-wage paychecks coming in the door! I don't know about you, but that's not a life that I want to live in. I'm only on this world for a short time - I want to live it up, not tie myself to a pole paying off debt for years to come.

The power of entrepreneurship and financial freedom is what's saving me from this mess I would otherwise be subjecting myself to. Using these same tips and tricks, many of them used by the most successful high-performing teens in the world, you can get ahead of the game and start doing what you want to do.

For you to really get how you can use the economy to your advantage, we need to go over a few topics to give you a clear understanding of what's going on. The first significant concept to understand is the general concept of money itself.

Currency

Before we had physical currency, society operated on a barter system.

If I wanted to get a chicken, and I had a rice farm, then I'd have to go find the chicken guy and trade him some rice. But what if the chicken guy already had rice, and what he really needed was wheat? The burden would be on me to go and find someone who wanted to trade wheat for my rice. It was a huge, complicated mess.

Money changed all of that by being something of a universal equalizer. Instead of going on a wild goose chase to get a chicken, I could just hand the chicken guy a slip of paper, or a piece of copper shaped into a coin, and he could spend it on whatever he wanted. This made the system easier, right?

Money - those slips of paper and those numbers on the quotrons on Wall Street, is the true basis of all human life. Without it, we'd crumble and resort to violence to get what we need.

It's long been the human dream to rack up as much money as possible. So how can we go ahead and do that?

As with all things in the world of money, the first step is to do some math. This type of math is fun, though, because it plots out exactly what you need to do to get a million dollars.

Do you need to sell 50,000 $20 products?

What about 20 $50,000 products?

Should you build a business that sells $114 in product, every 60 minutes, for an entire year?

How about getting 5,000 people to pay $17/mo for access to your online service?

Those are very realistic goals for someone who puts their mind to it. A million dollars doesn't seem so out of reach now, does it? You don't quite see the light at the end of the tunnel, but you at least know you're heading in the right direction.

Statistically, even if you decide to have a stable, average job, you'll reach at least $1 million dollars in income over your lifetime. The goal is to shorten the time it takes to earn that million as much as possible. You should aim to earn $1 million dollars every 10 years. Then earn $1 million dollars every year. Every quarter. Every month. Every day. So on and so forth.

Not only is this completely possible for students to do, but I personally know of dozens of teen entrepreneurs that can be placed into a similar math formula.

One of them runs a candy line that, at age 15, she's gotten into national brands like Whole Foods, Kroger, and Walmart. For her, selling $114 of her product an hour isn't just a guarantee - it's an indication that something's going horribly wrong, because she regularly does 10x that.

Income

The second significant concept to understand is the concept of income. Income is money you earn, whether from a job, a business, a gift, etc. To achieve a life of financial freedom, you need to increase your types of income so it can work for you. The ideal setup is to create sources of *passive* income that act as a 24/7 money generating machine!

We talked a bit about passive income - money you earn that doesn't require ongoing physical labor. On the other hand, active income is the type that most teenagers are familiar with. Working 20 hours per week at McDonald's is a form of active income, since it requires ongoing physical labor.

The overall concept for achieving financial freedom that I'm going to take you through, what I like to call the FFC (Financial Freedom Cycle), focuses on maximizing the amount of passive income you earn. This can be through the business you decide to start with the help of this book, a company you already own, and even just a normal job!

The FFC has to do entirely with income - creating as much of it as possible, increasing it, investing it wisely, and multiplying the flows of it. The FFC relies on the amount of monthly income you earn, not your "net worth", or one time deposits in your bank account.

There is no way you can make enough money to be considered "financially free" without making money month over month.

If you get an inheritance from your grandfather or uncle, that's great! You should invest that, but you shouldn't plan to live off of it. Your job is far from over.

That's because an inheritance is a one-time payment. Sure, your "net worth", whatever that means, will spike up, but at the end of the day, that money will end. Where will you be when it does?

Net passive cash flow is a much more valuable indicator of wealth than net worth. Net worth is basically useless as we enter into the 21st century - it's a number used to massage the egos of wealthy individuals, and is used as bragging rights in between groups of wealth.

Let's look at how net worth is traditionally calculated. Odds are you are not married yet at this young age, so let's assume for tax purposes, you are single.

Say you have a car that's worth $5,000, an investment portfolio your parents gave you worth $7,500, a savings account worth $1,200, and other material assets (Playstation, Computer, TV, etc.) valued at $2,500. You make roughly $24,000 per year at your part time job.

Let's also say you're a trust-fund kid (no college tuition), and your expenses are $1,800/mo. Your net worth, as traditionally calculated, would be:

$$(\$5,000 + \$7,500 + \$1,200 + \$2,500 + \$24,000) - (\$1,800 * 12)$$

Your traditional net worth would be $18,600 USD.

However, this is wrong. Why? Because this doesn't represent anything of actual value to someone striving to become financially free. It doesn't show you how you will survive on a month-to-month basis, and it doesn't account for the real value of your material assets.

Who determines the value of your car? Your Playstation, computer and TV? Are you even planning to sell those?

Let's calculate by a more realistic indicator - net passive cash flow. You have $2,000 per month coming into your bank account, with $1,800 per month of expenses. That now means that the amount of money you have coming in the door that you can invest is $200. That's a big jump from $18,600!

A commitment to growing your monthly income, either through your business, or if you're not ready to commit to taking the entrepreneurial jump, your job, is the biggest thing that can lead to financial freedom.

Take this hypothetical scenario for a second. Let's say you found a video game you really liked, but couldn't afford it. You loaded it on a credit card. Fast-forward 30 days, what happens when you can't make the payment?

Is it an issue that you bought an item that was too expensive?

It's not.

It's not an issue that you bought an item you liked - it's because you didn't make enough income in that month to cover that payment. That's a 100% preventable issue.

The only way you'll make enough money to buy that painting, that car, that thing you want more than anything, is to increase your income.

If you're in college, what are your monthly expenses? $1,800? $2,400? $3,700?

Jeff Bezos, one of the richest men alive, earns $2,400 every single second, whether he's awake or asleep. And there's not a whole lot of difference between him and you.

Sure, he may have a "smarter" mind, but he's still the same sack of flesh, bones, and blood that you are. He's just one that solved a smaller problem, and turned it into a bigger problem. (He started with books, now he sells everything).

95% of your time should be focused on generating income in any form. To really commit to a life of financial freedom, to achieve that goal of retiring early, or to get that expensive thing you really want, you need to commit to generating income.

Of the time you spend on your financial career, only 5% should be dedicated to expenses. The rest should be towards thinking about how you can make the most money possible, invest the most money possible, and achieve a path to financial freedom the fastest.

The first step of the FFC is to create income, and as much of it as possible. You'll certainly have better luck with starting your own business - I can make sure of that, but if you're not ready, find a job! Get a side-gig! Do whatever it takes to start getting money flowing in the door.

Once you have a steady flow of income every two weeks, your job is to do anything in your power to increase it even more. Obviously, this is a lot easier if you find an income source that's commission based, like sales, but not a lot of teens do.

If you find yourself lucky enough to be in that position, then you should work your ass off to make as much money on commission as possible.

However, as said, not a lot of teens find themselves in a commission-based environment, either self-employed or otherwise. That's perfectly normal, but limits what we have to work with. In that case, you should be on the look-out for any way to generate active income, like selling your old belongings, doing a quick side-gig, or even getting a second job. When we get to talk about taxes, claiming exemptions and deductions are another easy way to earn income.

Your main frame of mind in this step should be "How can I make as much money as possible?". You're on a clock here. The more time that money spends invested, the more money you can potentially make. Continuously seize opportunities to increase your income.

At Howdy Interactive, I know that people on our team drive for Uber, have a part-time job, and are active in the buy/sell/trade communities on online marketplaces. This isn't because I pay horribly (we're actually proud to have one of the highest starting pay for high school students in the United States, starting at $25/hr), but because they all know the importance of earning as much income as possible.

They don't want to be stuck with me for eternity! They want to go live on a beach in the Bahamas, so they're earning as much money as they can now to prepare them for this moment.

Bitching and moaning about "not having enough time", or "this not being fun" aren't valid excuses. Nobody said retiring early, and subsequently achieving a state of financial freedom would be easy. The idea is you start this process early so you can enjoy significantly more time off later in life. Whatever it takes, keep going. You need to create prosperity for yourself.

Committing to increasing your income doesn't have to be life-altering, but it should be an important part of your life. Send me new clients and I'll pay you! That's a great form of income. If your parents, friends, family, or somebody you know runs a business and needs marketing help, I'll send you a check for $3,000 when we close a deal for our monthly retainer marketing program. My contact information is plastered around this book, feel free to send 'em over.

Investing

When you have a substantial amount of income, the next step of the FFC is to invest it all. This is where most people fuck up, because they have an instant-gratification mentality. They did the hard work, so they should reap the rewards. Right?

Wrong.

Everything you've done, and everything you'll continue to do is so you can live a better life in the future. It's important that you save your income so you can grow it. Getting more money and immediately blowing it leaves you exactly where you started.

Like I mentioned earlier, investing is one of the most popular forms of generating passive income. Passive income - earning money in your sleep - is the way that you'll generate most of the money that will pave your path to financial freedom.

Now is a great time to introduce the third critical concept. Along with money and income, it's important that you know the general concepts of investing.

Hello! My lawyer has asked me to include a quick disclaimer.

When talking about investments, I'm talking about things that have worked for me. As with all investment opportunities, you should only put in what you're willing to lose. This book may make forward-looking statements about my organization (Howdy Interactive) and other investment strategies. Please make your investment decisions based off of already available products and information.

I'd advise you to consult with your family's financial planner, CPA, and/or lawyer if you have questions.

Investment, according to the dictionary, is the act of allocating funds to an entity, with the expectation of generating an income or profit.

The aforementioned entity could be a number of things. It could be a stock, which is a singular company's raised capital based on the value of their shares. It could be an ETF, which diversifies its portfolio by investing in more than one asset. It could be a piece of real estate, or an investment into a real estate fund. It could also be an investment back into your own company!

Take a look at Dunkin' Donuts, for example. They're taking $0.15 of coffee, and reselling it for $3.50 to millions of people on a daily basis. However, before they could get away with that, they had to invest in land, construction, an infrastructure, branding, inventory, franchise management, and staff to run all of their locations.

To become financially free, you need to earn and invest income. Just doing one won't help. You won't get rich investing all of your assets if you only have $100. However, you won't get rich just by making money. Nicholas Cage earned tens of millions of dollars, and promptly spent it all on useless nonsense, including, and this is true, **a gothic castle.**

He didn't bother to invest any of his money, and now he's in debt.

A strategy you can employ to help you start thinking about investing all of your funds is something called the "Two Bank Accounts" rule. Each one of your entities should only have two bank accounts. You, as an individual, should only have two bank accounts - a checking account and a savings account. Your business should only have two bank accounts - a business checking and a business saving account.

Your checking account should be used for the majority of your day-to-day expenses. Charge everything to a credit card, or if you can't get one, a debit card. Paired with a budgeting software like Mint, it's a deadly personal finance tool that you can use to your advantage.

Keeping track of every penny you spend is super important, because it allows you to "trim the fat" and cut out unnecessary items. The more you trim out of your budget now, the more you can add to investment accounts and watch it grow later.

The savings account should be seldom used. Unforeseen things come up, and you might need a safe place to move your money if your checking account information gets leaked. However, you should not use your savings account to actively store money inside of it. You should look at your savings account every day and think, "How can I get rid of all of this money?"

As much of your money as possible should be in investments. If you're saving for a trip, or a rainy day fund, then invest your money in a safer fund, like the S&P 500. It's a significantly diluted risk than, say, investing in a real estate fund, and as such it will generate less money.

However, generating less money is better than generating no money.

Say you need $600 for a weekend getaway, and you hold that $600 in the bank for three months before your trip. Holding it in a traditional savings account, at a generous .5% APY (Annual Percentage Yield), you'll earn about $0.75 in interest over those three months.

Now, if you decide to invest your $600 for your trip in a fund like the S&P 500, at the end of those three months, you'll have about $615.13 (based on past market data).

It takes about two seconds of work to decide which account you'll transfer funds into - savings, or investment. There's nothing special about this process that's off-limits to teen entrepreneurs. With parental permission, we can invest just the same as everyone.

So why would you settle for less, when for the exact same physical effort, you could have an extra burrito, or a few extra drinks? Taking that saved money and investing it into a low-risk investment, instead of stuffing it into another savings account, generates you free money and is the basis of achieving financial freedom - having your money work for you.

Now, if you wanted to take a gamble and start investing your trip's funds into some riskier investments, you can certainly earn more money. However, the risk is significantly greater and you up your chances of losing your investment.

It's common sense - higher risk, higher reward.

Legally, I'm required to continuously tell you that I'm not a financial planner - I'm just sharing strategies that work for me as somebody rather close to your position.

I don't know your specific Netflix viewing habits, but if you haven't seen it already, I recommend watching Narcos. It's about Pablo Escobar, the ruthless Colombian drug lord that butchers, executes, and tortures anyone who gets in his way, as well as their friends and family. It's a fantastic, realistic depiction of the Medellin drug cartel.

Unfortunately, Pablo had a serious problem. He had a lot of money. A lot of it. Billions and billions of dollars. In fact, he had so much money, he couldn't physically store it all.

He tried everything he could, it just was too much money. With no other alternatives, he started burying it in the ground.

Very quickly, the cash started to get moldy and wet, and the termites attacked shortly thereafter. The cash was now useless.

Assuming you don't run a drug smuggling cartel, your money should be clean and you shouldn't have an issue using legitimate measures to grow your money.

If your cash sits in a bank, it's doing absolutely nothing. It'll take about 40 years to get a 10% return on your investment for average savings accounts in the United States. That is not a good path to financial freedom.

Let's look at two better options. First, we need to define two terms: "Accredited Investor", and "Non-Accredited" Investor.

A non-accredited investor is a regular person. There are a few restrictions on what they can invest in, but for the most part, they are able to buy and sell stocks, ETFs, and mutual funds, just like anybody else.

An accredited investor has no investment restrictions, and can also invest traditionally in private corporations, investment funds, and REITs (real estate investment trust). Your goal is to get into this bracket as quickly as possible so you can have those investing restrictions removed.

The average rate of return for the S&P 500, a collection of valuable stocks, is 10% on an annual basis. I'm not going to give advice on specific stocks here because that's a very slippery legal slope, and I've already broken an elbow going down that road.

I would recommend you move forward with opening an investment account with Vanguard. I used them for my investments, before I switched to something better (we'll talk about that in a minute!)

The good news is, however, we've gone from an average 0.25% return (sitting in a savings account), to an average 10% annual return. Talk about 10Xing your income - we've just 40Xed the passive income that your money makes!

"But Nathan," you ask, "You just said that there's something better! Why are you saving the best for yourself?"

That's a great question. There's something that's better than the stock market, something that produces a whopping 15% average annual return - 60X the amount of money you would have gotten by having your funds sit in a bank.

That something is real estate.

You might be wondering, "Well how do I go about investing in real estate?!?!? I don't have enough money for that!"

Most teens might not, but the bar to entering the real estate investment market is very low for everybody, including non-accredited investors.

For as little as $5,000, you can invest in a real estate investment fund. My preferred fund is Cardone Capital, but there are plenty of alternatives out there.

What these funds do is they find apartment buildings, gated communities, anything where people can pay monthly rent. The partners in the fund become partners in the actual real estate (this isn't a REIT or a stock). They collect rent and manage the properties, and they send you cash dividends.

Stocks are pieces of paper traded in the big world of business. It's prone to financial collapses, as we saw in 1929, and more recently, in 2008. There are lots of people who have made money with the stock market, but there are just as many stories about people who lost everything they owned.

From a starter's perspective, it's perfect, though - it'll get you up and running.

Everyone needs a place to stay. Investing in real estate will mean that you're prepared to make a move when the next recession hits, because your fund will still be collecting rent and paying you monthly dividends.

Personally, I have all of my money in a real estate fund, and I would recommend it to any teens who have enough upfront capital to make a move on it.

However, if you're just starting out, and have a smaller amount to invest, stocks, mutual funds, and ETFs have a pretty good annual return as well.

At the end of the day, it really just depends on your own investment strategy. I would ask your parents and local mentors how they handle their money, and how they're investing to get some ideas on your specific situation.

One thing I would advise you not to do, as well as most sane financial planners, is invest in cryptocurrency.

Do you remember December 2017?

Bitcoin grew from 1 BTC = $10,930.24 USD on December 1st, to being worth 1 BTC = $19,650.01 USD on December 15th.

In 14 days, people literally doubled their money. Those who had invested a mere $50,000 now had $89,855.39.

Exactly 1 year later, on December 15th 2018, that $50,000 investment was worth $14,557.53. The value of Bitcoin plummeted, and people lost a lot of money. In fact, some people even committed suicide because the amount of money they lost was just so high.

Don't put yourself in this position - NEVER, EVER invest in trends! Warren Buffet's number one rule of investing is to never, ever lose money. These are all trends - they will come and go and you will be none the wiser, but your pocket will be emptier.

I stayed out of Bitcoin and cryptocurrency, and when Rally Road announced they were selling shares of expensive cars, I stayed out of that as well!

I started with stocks, funds, and ETFs because they're somewhat concrete - a lot more concrete than most trends like Rally Road and Crypto. Then, I found something better, real estate, and switched over to exclusively investing in real estate funds (Note: NOT REITs!)

Multiply Income Flows

When you have a hold on the investment step of the FFC (Financial Freedom Cycle), we can move on to the final step, which is increasing your income flows. Whether that means diversifying your investment portfolio, mining Bitcoin, getting another job, or earning royalties on something, that's your next step.

If you depend on just a single income flow and if it gets cut-off, or fails (like a financial crisis), you're entirely screwed.

You hear about so many people getting laid off from their jobs, or a business's inventory getting destroyed in a fire, but you never think about it yourself. The truth is, you never know what can happen to you, your products, or your job.

You should always have a second source of income so you can use it as a life raft while you recover from the loss of the first source of income shutting down. Even better, when things go smoothly, you now have a second source of income that you can expand and grow, speeding the time it'll take you to achieve financial freedom. You should never tap into your investments at a point of emergency - always tap into your second income sources. Like I said, Warren Buffet's first rule of investing is to never lose money.

If you're not at the point where you want to start your own business, that's perfectly fine - there are still ways to have two sources of income, but you may need to split your time.

If you work a full-time, 40-hour per week job, swap it out for two 20-hour per week jobs. If you work a part-time, 20-hour per week jobs, swap them out for two 10-hour per week jobs.

Alternatively, you can also become a freelancer or start a small side-hustle, outsourcing what you do for work to other people for a higher price. Plenty of people become cyber-security consultants, publishing consultants, tax consultants, etc.

I would ask you to re-invest the money (because investing your dividends and expendable income is the fastest way to financial freedom), but if you're at the point where you can still grow your financial empire while still paying for your living expenses, that's great to hear and exactly what we're looking for.

As a teen, by picking up this book, you walked into this situation with a remarkable goal - earning enough money to be financially free by the time you graduate college. That's compressing about 50 years of work into 8 years or less, depending on where you are in high school and/or college.

While it's certainly possible, and the FFC system will help you tremendously, it'll take hard work. Luckily, you're in good hands. The FFC is based on the advice and lessons of myself and dozens of the world's most prominent teen entrepreneurs, coupled with strategies and methodologies from billionaires and extraordinarily wealthy individuals.

It makes no sense to copy the investment strategy of a billionaire at an early age, because their investment portfolio is largely defensive. You need to play offense - racking up as much money as possible, as quickly as possible. Then you can worry about making sure your investments are nice and safe.

Playing offense is a good segue into the fourth concept that you should understand as a teen entrepreneur, which is some of the tools that will help you climb the path to financial freedom.

Credit

The first one, and one of the most important tools, is the concept of credit. In day-to-day life, you see this most commonly with credit cards. Credit is a promise you make to a lender (known as the creditor) to pay them back, sometimes with extra fees, in exchange for gaining access to money before you have it in the bank (known as a line of credit).

I personally use the 20/30/50 budget, which works very well for me, and uses credit cards to the maximum. I have two actively used personal credit cards, a checking account, and a savings account. I told you I reap what I sow!

20% of my personal income is dedicated towards personal expenses - the fun stuff like movies, eating out, Netflix, books, etc. That's what my first credit card is used for. I've set the credit limit to cap at 20% of my income, and have instructed my credit card company not to raise it without my permission.

The second credit card is for all of my essential expenses, like food, transportation, etc. If I can't pay a specific bill by card, something you'll see a lot with older companies, I use a service like PLASTIQ that allows me to pay them by credit card, and they send a check or wire transfer on my behalf. It keeps my accounting in one place - on my credit card statement. 30% of my personal income is dedicated to this.

Finally, the other 50% of my income is dedicated towards my investments in real estate. I save it all and don't touch it, ever.

Credit cards don't generally get a good reputation, but why exactly is that? I have three of 'em - two for personal and one for business. They're fantastic. I rack up points, cash back, and have never had a debt issue with a credit card company.

Everyone uses them, from people like you and me all of the way up to billionaires, small businesses, and Fortune 500 companies. I guarantee you that if there was a real issue with credit cards, no wealthy person would use them. It's not the card that's the problem, but how you use it.

A tactic that I use is to treat all of my credit cards like employees. Just like your employees need to get paid every month, so do your cards. In exchange for getting them paid, they work for me by providing a statement I can send to my accountant, and racking up rewards that come with the card.

Pay off your cards every month. Don't spend more than you know that you're going to earn in cash flow that moth. Don't tap into your investments, ever, to pay off your cards. That money is for growth, not for bailing you out of your poor financial choices.

Tax Avoidance

The other important tool that you have in your "Financial Freedom Arsenal" is tax avoidance. Notice I didn't say "tax evasion", which is a crime. However, avoiding paying your taxes by claiming deductions, exemptions, and deferrals is very legitimate and very legal. It's how you hear stories every year about Amazon.com paying no taxes to the IRS.

I'm personally not a fan of how the government uses my money, regardless of who's in the Oval Office, so I make it a point to pay as little taxes as possible.

> Another reminder - please talk with your family's CPA before you do anything drastic, or if you have any questions!

A term you should know by heart is your "tax burden", or "tax liability". It's basically the amount of taxes you need to pay. Please note that this section talks about federal taxes, not state or local taxes. Those are three very different tax bills.

Your entire focus going into the "world of taxes" should be to pay as much money to the IRS as possible. At first, this seems counter-intuitive. Why would I want to work hard to give all of my money to Uncle Sam? However, if you walk in thinking that you should be working to pay the IRS as little as possible, your brain won't want to make as much money as you need to become financially free. Financial freedom is only achievable by committing to increasing your income.

When it's tax season and you've focused on paying the IRS as much as possible, and in-turn, generating as much money for yourself as possible, you have two options for success here.

The first option you can take is by reducing your overall tax burden through deductions. The second option is to defer your tax burden to a later date, where you'll have more cash flow to make another move.

You can reduce your overall tax burden in a number of ways. The easiest is to deduct items for your business. If you're planning on starting a business, head to your state's Secretary of State website and create a formal LLC or corporation. This will make it easier for yourself as you move into the next few chapters about starting & scaling your company. When you own a business on the books, you can go to town.

The IRS is very business-friendly. If you know how to use it right, you can significantly reduce your tax burden.

For example...

- If you use your vehicle for work, like traveling to a client, or going to a conference, or picking up supplies, be sure to track the miles you travel professionally - they're tax deductible. Better yet, if your credit score allows, try to lease your vehicle instead of buying it. If you use the vehicle 25% of the time for your business, you can deduct 25% of the lease on your taxes.

- If you feel inclined to buy a vehicle, and can justify using it more than 50% of the time for work, get a van or a pickup truck! I personally have a pickup truck. Vehicles classified as heavy automobiles get a tax credit, and can be written off in their entirety under Section 179.

- If you pay rent and have a home workspace (like a spare second bedroom) in your apartment, you can deduct a portion of your rent. Furthermore, everything you buy for your home workspace is classified as a business expense, and can be written off under 26 CFR § 1.162-1.

The deductions go on and on! For your specific situation, I'd recommend consulting with your family attorney, or really any CPA. They'll be able to point out some more tips and tricks, but hopefully this gets your mind spinning.

If you're a little short for cash, you might want to look into deferring your tax burden. Let's say this year you make $50,000 - a marvelous feat in of itself, since most students make 3x less than that. Of that $50k, about $20,000 is taxable and can't be deducted. You don't have $20,000 in liquid assets to go and buy a car and write it off - perfectly understandable when you're starting out. What you can do is defer the tax burden so you can make more money in the meantime.

You can claim up to nine exemptions/allowances on your W-4. This has nothing to do with the amount of people who depend on you, which you might have heard you can claim tax credits for in your tax return. What this does is reduces the amount of money that your employer (or your business!) holds on each of your paychecks. You're still eligible to get taxed on this money, which is why it's a deferral and not a deduction.

However, instead of sitting in another bank account waiting to be taken to Uncle Sam, it can be in one of your low-risk investment funds, earning you money while you sleep.

Holding your investments for a long period of time is also a great way to defer taxes. Not all taxes are deferrable, but there are certainly some options that are only taxable when you take control of the profit.

Even though I've delved previously into what I keep my money in, this book isn't structured to give you specific investment advice because it's such a slippery slope. The aim of this book is to show you how teen entrepreneurs around the world are scaling their path to financial freedom.

I have one last thought to share before we wrap up the first chapter.

Enjoying Success

My favorite book I was forced to read in high school was The Great Gatsby by F. Scott Fitzgerald. If you're not familiar, it's a story about how a young man, Jay Gatsby, from the West Egg of Long Island, tries to chase his true love, Daisy, who lives on the East Egg.

The difference between the two is that the East Egg is classified as "old money" - they grew up and have been around money their entire life. Jay Gatsby is a "new money" guy - someone who earned his own fortune.

West Egg people tend to throw amazing parties, drive expensive cars, and show off/flaunt their wealth.

The first time you have money in your pocket, the first few thousand dollars you make from your business that are all yours, you'll want to show off - you made it.

You'll want to pick up meal tabs, go on expensive vacations, stay in the best hotels, tip ridiculously high, etc. I went through it, my entrepreneurial friends went through it, even the big shots went through it. Steve Jobs got a Gulfstream V jet, valued at $44 million dollars.

However, making a few thousand dollars isn't exactly the definition of "financial freedom". Don't fool yourself by living the good life for a few weeks. Eventually, you'll need to go back to work to replenish your bank account.

And when the next paycheck comes in, you'll want to invest a little bit more of your money, instead of spending it immediately.

Then with your next deposit, a little more, and then a little more...

Because you're going to notice that while staying in luxurious hotels, and getting massages, and eating the best good is fantastic, there's one thing that you're going to want more than anything in the world.

It might be a house. I have a dream house - 822 Sarbonne Road in Bel Air, CA, valued at $75,000,000.

It might be a car. I have a dream car - A light purple Rolls Royce Dawn, valued at $650,000.

It might even be a plane. Above anything else in the world, I want a private jet - a Gulfstream G450, valued at $23,500,000.

Those are some goals that you can only achieve with true financial freedom. You're not going to get there with a few thousand dollars. It's a good start, but it's exactly that: A Start.

So go ahead and celebrate your success! Send me a postcard from any exotic destination you go to. (Seriously, send me postcards to my office: 2 Hammond Street, Floor 3, Bangor ME 04401 USA).

But remember that when you come back from vacation, you're going to have to kick ass to make sure you keep living this lifestyle.

Chapter 2: Mindset

Your mindset is very important when thinking about money, business, and expanding your empire. Think about how committed the visionary founders are: Elon Musk, Steve Jobs, Jeff Bezos, etc.

"To those of you who are graduating this afternoon with high honors, awards, and distinctions, I say 'Well done.' And as I like to tell the C students, 'You too, can be president'."
- President George W. Bush

"Don't be a little bitch" - Grant Cardone

"If they say it's impossible, it means it's impossible for them, not for you." - Anonymous

Have you noticed something about successful people? Their mindset is completely different than the normal person. They long for success, and they have the drive, motivation, and stamina to see their goal through. Drive is what powered some of the world's most successful people to get where they are today.

Just as successful people have a different mindset, high-performing teens - the great athletes, performers, dancers, and yes, entrepreneurs - are completely different than students looking for day-to-day stability and security.

The way they function is different than the status-quo. Sure, they might do the same things - attend practice, eat the same food as you, watch Netflix, etc. - but the actions are only half the battle. If you approach a situation like achieving financial freedom by just "going through the motions", you'll get absolutely nowhere.

Here's a less-than-fun-fact: Did you know that nearly 48% of Americans don't have even $400 in their checking account, and nothing in their investment account?

Most people are just struggling to get by, let alone thrive and soar. The fact that, at such a young age, you're looking to do so - it's a bit of a leap from the world you might be used to. I'm not saying that's bad! However, you may feel dumb, funny, or stupid striving for excellence and financial freedom. The insecurity is real - and it doesn't just affect people starting out.

I was at a mastermind in Boston, attending with a few other fellow teen entrepreneurs. Over dinner, we morphed into a discussion about their starting stories - how did they get their start in entrepreneurship at such a young age? One of my friends asked "How many of you doubted yourself severely when you were starting out?"

Everybody at the table raised their hands.

"How many are doubting yourself on a daily basis right now?"

Everyone kept their hands up.

That's because I think there hasn't been a good resource yet on the correct mindset you need to achieve financial freedom. I'm not saying that this book is the one, but rather than giving you some bullshit overview of how you can have a "winner's mindset", or spending time convincing you to do a "life overhaul", I want to talk about some specific strategies that teen entrepreneurs around the world have employed to jumpstart their success stories.

Implementing these should give you a head-start. Not only in the world of business, but in every aspect of your life - dealing with academics, family, extra-curriculars, and your friendships/relationships.

The first concept is all about priming your mind. Unless you're in a JROTC-esque program, or otherwise preparing for the military, this is probably the biggest change you'll have to make. It deals with the way you approach tackling projects in your life, and how you can use this strategy as you begin to scale your business.

The second concept is hacking a well-known organizational methodology to get more shit done in a shorter time period. The ability to do more in less time unlocks the ability for you to perform at a higher level than your peers in every aspect of your life by default.

The third concept is somewhat of a different look at the world of education. It trains you to learn about things that will help you later in life, in a way that doesn't actually feel like learning. In case you're like me and hate school, it won't leave you feeling bored or annoyed that you're learning something.

Finally, the fourth concept, is going to be about one of the largest entertainment companies in the world, and how you can model their commitment to customer experience and attention to detail. Getting a handle on this will allow you to create more value in your relationships, whether they're with your peers, your family, or eventually, your customers.

There are plenty of books and resources that are very famous that I'm sure one of your parents tried to get you to read. The most famous culprit of this is the 7 Habits of Highly Effective Teens. It walks you through seven habits that "set you up for success", and helps you create a mission statement for your life.

Who the fuck wants to do that? I want to make money, not spend time "finding my values". That comes later when I actually have money and want to scale.

You should not be reading this book if you don't want to. If climbing the path to financial freedom through teen entrepreneurship doesn't sound like your thing, that's not a problem - it's not for everyone. Put the book down and go do something else.

The tips in this book are reserved for people who actually want to achieve success early-on in life, just like the dozens of teens who have done it already, and in a broader view, the millions of millionaires around the world.

The information I want to impart on you is purely based on content that teens can actually change in their lives to set themselves up for success, without feeling overwhelmed or bored. If this sounds good to you, let's get started.

Self-Discipline

Peter Thiel says that the common millionaire - a person who has $1,000,000 in liquid assets, can't even provide proper legal defense for his family.

With less than $400, as we found out before that most Americans don't even have, you can't even change a flat tire, let alone defend yourself from a lawsuit.

There are two types of people. People who are willing to sit there and let life screw them over, and those who are willing to do something about it.

You, I believe, are part of the latter group. However, you need to watch out for people who will drag you down.

Connor Blakley, teen marketing juggernaut, says, "When you're trying to do big things, people with small minds feel like they're getting attacked. Big ideas make small minds feel inferior."

It may be comfortable to stay at mediocrity. Sure, you can go home every night and play World of Warcraft, or binge the latest Netflix show. But here's the thing - if you stay average, you're just going to be a springboard for someone who wants it more than you.

You'll be an addition to another statistic; you'll help move the statistics on the amount of Americans without $400 from 48% to 49%. To motivated teens who want to actually to achieve success, you'll just be a springboard for them.

I don't want that for you, and deep down, you don't want that for yourself.

You picked up this book for a reason, and it's bigger than you just "running a business" as a teenager. In most cases, it's to make some changes. Whatever you want: money, power, influence, sex, friendships, favors, drugs, it doesn't matter.

Financial freedom is your gateway to above the world of mediocrity. If you don't take this chance, someone else will gladly take your place.

I'm going to steal Grant Cardone's methodology - you need to 10X your thinking.

Chances are, if you attend high school right now, the focus is on preparing you for the workforce. They don't teach you to think big.

A lot of teachers say that the highest you can go, the most money you can make, is by being a lawyer or a doctor. You can put in the work, and eventually make $250,000 per year.

Fuck that. I want to make $2,500,000 per month, not $250,000 per year. 10X your thinking, and 10X the actions you take to get where you want to go.

If you want to start a business, if you really want things to change, you need to commit to this 100%. Ignore everyone who says you can't do it; that it's impossible. Them saying it's impossible means it's impossible to them, not to you.

With your ambitious (and realistic) goals, some people will drop out of your life. Some people will hate you and everything you stand for. They won't understand why you can't settle.

Try to explain yourself, but don't waste too much time on it. Remember what I said in the first chapter - 95% of your time should be spent on income, 5% on expenses. Arguing about the state of your business is certainly an expense of your energy.

As you get farther into the development of your business, perhaps when you make the first $15,000 or the first $25,000, right around there you'll find someone who will try to fuck you over.

They might be jealous. They might think you stole their idea. There may not be a reason for it. I've had people try and sabotage everything from my live events to company trips.

Be aware of people like that, and don't associate with them. Cut off the "friendship" before it gets dangerous - not physically, but to the way of life you're trying to create. It's better to lose one "friend" than it is to lose a life of financial freedom.

When stuff like that happens, just report it to the police and move on. Have a zero-tolerance policy for people trying to screw you over, and you'll notice the amount of people who try to do it will fall considerably.

Embarking on the path to financial freedom is largely a mental challenge.

How many teenagers, 19 years old and younger, do you know that have more than $1 million dollars in self-earned assets? I know 27 of them, and 14 more than will hit that goal in the next three months.

Do you know how they've achieved such a high level of success?

They committed to the challenge mentally. They made it their number one priority in life to "live the good life". Nothing came above this goal of making money.

You might think that it's too harsh, or you can get away with less of a commitment, but you honestly can't. If you want to retire by the time you graduate college, or even shortly thereafter, you are condensing five decades of work into a few years.

This is trading working super hard for a few years so you can enjoy the rest of your life, versus working the average amount for decades and decades, so you can only enjoy a few years at the end.

Theoretically, this can work for longer/less work periods - you could put in 75% effort and retire by the time you're 30, etc. I don't recommend it - go big or go home. Bill Gates said he didn't take a day off from work, not even a single one, between his 20th and 30th birthdays.

If you want to be a billionaire, follow his advice. I'm not the richest person in the world, so I can't help you if your goal is world domination. What I can help you with, however, is becoming financially free. That means making enough money where you're happy. That number is probably a bit lower than whatever Bill Gates is worth right now.

Self-discipline is the first concept because it powers the days where your drive and motivation to get to financial freedom is non-existent.

Instead of motivation powering you through those days, it's pure discipline - so you continually work on the things you're supposed to, not because you want to that day, but because you know that it'll help you live a better life in the future.

It takes the same amount of time, money, and energy to think big as it does to think small. Since you can think big anyway, why not go ahead and just do what you need to do?

You need to think about your priorities right now. What's important to you? You can't do everything. Is it crafting a life of financial freedom? Great! Is it sports, or getting into a top college? That's fine too. Is it academics? Fantastic.

You only have enough mental power to really focus on two priorities at a time. If you take a long, hard look at yourself and figure out that entrepreneurship isn't for you, that's fine! You can still use the FFC cycle from the money chapter to earn more income than your peers, even if you're in a job - at least this wasn't a total lost cause.

However, the more of a priority you make achieving a life of financial freedom, the better you'll set yourself up for success.

I talk a lot about financial freedom, as you can probably tell, because I think it's the ultimate goal. Whatever you want can be realistically achieved with cold, hard cash in your pocket.

Get into a good college? Bribe someone. Do it better than Felicity Huffman did. Want access to some of the most successful people in the world?

Donate to their foundation. Want to make even more money? It takes money to make money.

However, to begin the path to financial freedom, you need to change your mindset about success a little bit.

It takes more to be a millionaire than just saying "Alright, today I decide I want to be a millionaire!".

Sure, that's how it starts, but you need to commit to the idealism of saving and investing money.

If you wanted to be the world's best actor, soccer player, chef, whatever - you wouldn't say, "Alright, I want to be the best!" and just leave it at that.

You'd have to practice, take classes, learn, and add to your arsenal of knowledge. You'd have to break down the barrier to anything disposable in your life that you can get rid of. You'd have to do so even on days that you didn't feel like doing it - you'd have to push on and achieve your goal.

Becoming financially free is no different than training to be the best actor, soccer player, or chef - you're training to be the best entrepreneur in the world.

I want to make something clear - I'm not saying to remove yourself from day-to-day life.

If you place a high priority on academics, of course you shouldn't drop out! You shouldn't shut out all of your friends, you shouldn't stop working out, you shouldn't stop having relationships, etc.

But instead of coming home from school and binging Netflix, make some cold calls. Instead of skipping class to go smoke weed with your friends, skip to go to a client meeting.

Grant Cardone was in his thirties when he made his first million, and another $300 million after that. He was addicted to drugs until his mid-twenties, and started his business shortly thereafter.

He has often said that his one change, if he could go back and do everything differently, would be to get his shit together earlier in life.

Imagine where Grant Cardone would be now if he started thinking about business the way he does at age 16? Even age 22?

You have an advantage - you are starting to play this game early. Learning about the big world of business at an early age can only help you in life, it can't hurt you.

You might even be wondering, "Nathan, I think I have the right mindset now - when will we get to the fun stuff? About running an actual business?"

We'll get there! But everything past the Mindset chapter is completely useless if you can't commit to doing the work and trying to strive for a better life.

My only point of contact with you is through this book, and maybe through my podcast or blog. I only have a certain amount of time to drill this into your head before you're back in the real world, and I want to make sure I take advantage of all of the attention you've given me.

Do you know what else high-performing teens have in common? They don't make excuses. They don't (audibly) bitch and moan when they go to practice, or go rehearse their music, or go meet with client after client. They get up, get the work done, go above and beyond, and then go home and reap the rewards.

Making excuses is a loser's game, because the only one you're cheating is yourself and your chance at a better life.

I know this is easier said than done. If you need help with self-discipline, I would recommend looking into Jocko Willink.

He's a retired Navy SEAL that publishes a lot of content with self-discipline. He has a podcast and an audio tape, but his two flagship books are Extreme Ownership and Discipline Equals Freedom. I recommend you read both.

Whether or not you want to admit it, no matter what situation you are facing, the only reason that you are not performing at the level you want to be is because you have excuses that are weighing you down.

It's causing you to procrastinate, to doubt yourself, or to otherwise not commit to the action steps that will take you to where you want to go.

It's perfectly okay to doubt yourself, but it's not okay to procrastinate. Crush that before it gets out of control. Become hyper-aggressive, and just get it done.

You are the only person that can control yourself. It's a blessing and a curse wrapped up into one. You're not responsible for the actions of anyone else - your co-founders, your employees, your clients, your friends, your family - just you. But that also means that you're the only one on the hook for your actions.

If you truly want to change your situation, don't be a little bitch about it. Plow through the procrastination and the excuses. Play to 100% of your strength, and you'll get 100% of the results.

A big part of what helps me train my self-discipline is making my bed every day. I'm sure a lot of you have seen, or your teachers showed you the commencement speech given by Naval Admiral William McRaven, where he tells you to make your bed every morning.

Believe it or not, the simple act of making your bed can cause a "domino" effect of you being uber-productive.

Making your bed as soon as you get up is like accomplishing the first task of the day. Once it's done, you'll feel more comfortable doing something else, like making breakfast.

Then, making breakfast will make you feel more comfortable doing something else, like responding to emails. It's a chain reaction of productivity, and it works.

Before the day is through, that one simple task of making your bed in the morning would be the powering spark that helped you get many more tasks done that day.

Making your bed has additional benefits outside of testing your self-discipline stamina.

If your bed is nice and clean, it'll reflect positively on your bedroom, and neurologically relaxes you and your mind. Alongside the mental effects, a made-up bed will make your room look nicer, even if it's super dirty on the floor.

Finally, if life kicks your ass that day, whether in school or in business, you come home to a nice, made bed - a small silver lining at the end of a horrible day.

"Making your bed will also reinforce the fact that little things in life matter. If you can't do the little things right, you will never do the big things right." - Naval Admiral William McRaven

If you're still struggling with excuses, I want to cut through the bullshit and give you some real reasons that you have not taken steps to increase your income.

Academics

This is a bit of a hard one - our society has been programmed to analyze school as a top priority. But you are in a special situation here - you are an entrepreneur.

Remember I told you about Connor Blakley? He posted a Youtube video where he walked through his life as a teen entrepreneur, and he told us the story about how he was kicked out of his high school because of his excessive work traveling. The final straw was him going to meet the CEO of Sprint, and 10 minutes before the meeting, he got an email from the Head of School informing him he had to find another high school to study with.

I actually have a very similar story!

I founded Howdy Interactive in 9th grade, the year I started at Maine's most famous private high school. My grades suffered tremendously because of the work I put into my business, mostly influenced by my time away from school traveling for work. I received a letter from the Head of School over the summer that I was not invited back for a second year.

Funnily enough, I ran into him last year while Howdy was producing a live event worth three times his yearly salary.

The issue of balancing academics depends on how far along you are in your entrepreneurial pursuit, and how risky it is for you.

I would almost always recommend not to drop out of high school. This year, I am on Connections Academy, which is a public virtual charter school. It allows me to keep up with academics while traveling, working, and consulting with our clients.

However, college is a whole other story. Bill Gates, Steve Jobs, Mark Zuckerburg, etc. all dropped out of college, and it's very romanticized to try and follow in their footsteps.

You need to determine how successful you can be, and how large you can increase your income to. There's not a one-size fits all solution to balancing or removing academics from your plate.

However, you need to do what you can to minimize the amount of time and effort you spend on academics. This should be non-negotiable.

Using some of the techniques in the second concept, you'll be able to reduce some of your academic workload. Use that spare time to work on your business. If you're not willing to put your financial life ahead of your academic life, at least make it equal.

Entitlement

Perhaps living with a guardian who has taken care of the bills for you has had you wander off a little bit. Let me pull you back into reality with a quote from my favorite fictional character, Francis J. Underwood.

You are entitled to nothing.

If you think that good things will fall into your lap, you should take this book back and get a refund, because it's of no value to you.

Nobody has ever gotten rich accepting handouts, whether it's from the government, from your parents, or from a company.

Truly entitled people will never earn real money, because they feel that things should be given to them.

Entitled people don't have the work ethic that chasing the dream of financial freedom, and everything that I and this book preach, require.

Normal Action

Those who thrive on "normal action" will never get where you need to go. If you are fine with working

20-hour weeks, making $25k/yr, this is not the world for you.

The people who successfully achieve financial freedom, not just teen entrepreneurs, but the greats: Jobs, Bezos, Gates, Musk, Dell, Packard, Ford, etc. thrive on doing more than is expected.

Hell, Elon Musk basically sleeps on the floor of his office because he works so much!

You need to change your frame of mind. Instead of making 25 sales calls, do 150. Instead of sending out 10 emails at a time, send out 80.

By doing 2x, 5x, or even 10x the work, you'll reap more of the rewards than everyone else you're competing against, be it classmates, business competitors, etc.

Time Management

Even if you want, more than anything in the world, to climb the path to financial freedom, there's no way you'll be able to accomplish it without getting your head in the right place. These things are instrumental to every entrepreneur's workbook.

It is essential to get good time management habits! This is one of those things that if you screw it up, everyone can see. Your parents, teachers, clients, vendors, etc. - anybody you have appointments or deadlines with.

The average student is dealing with so much shit on a normal basis - school, friends, work, relationships, homework, etc. - that putting a business in the mix without any idea of how you manage your time with cripple your life.

Done right, a correct look at time management can allow you to completely change your life. It'll give you more time to focus on what's valuable to you. It's important to introduce the infrastructure of time management before you begin scaling your business, so you have the time to focus on everything going on in your life as your business begins to become more and more successful.

Before you start implementing time management strategies, I'm sure you can agree that they won't be useful if you don't know what your current day looks like. We need to conduct something called a "time audit".

Hop into a calendar software (the most popular by far is Google Calendar), and walk through your week. Start at the time you wake up, and slowly fill in the holes. Add in time slots for everything you normally do, like:

- The time you spend at school
- Your average dinner time
- How much homework you do on a daily basis, and
- What extracurriculars you have, and how much time they take up

Write your entire day down for the entire week, Monday through Sunday, and then step back and take a look. Chances are, the schedule is most likely not where you want it to be. There might be some holes, overlapping events, or an unrealistic bed time. That's alright!

Our goal is to now take this schedule and transform it into something that's functional and can accommodate starting and scaling a business.

When it comes to managing your workload, it's best to keep your personal, academic, and work lives all in one place so you can easily plot things out accordingly. The only tool I would recommend for this purpose is Basecamp.com, which allows you to contextualize your life through communication-based project management.

Basecamp has to-dos, check-ins, calendars, and other tools that can all connect with one another to give you an overview of your life. Usually, it's used exclusively for business, but Basecamp has also started catering towards overall personal use.

I use this tool for everything, including managing the production of this entire book. It was written, edited, published, and marketed using Basecamp.

I have the business plan for $99/mo, but you don't need that when starting out. They have a forever free version, which can set you up for life! You won't pay a dollar, ever, and they have an "until the end of the internet" guarantee that makes sure your data will still be here in the future. This is their 15th year in business, and they continue to grow.

Using a project management system allows you to have a birds-eye view of everything you do. It's perfect for seeing when you have spare time, what tasks you do are unnecessary, and what you need to dedicate more time to. Use it to track your academic work alongside your personal and business stuff, and I guarantee you that you'll start to see positive change in your grades.

The overall aim of time management is to squeeze as much productivity out of your day as possible, so you can perform at a higher level than your peers. The philosophy that a significant amount of teen entrepreneurs use is not doing more inside of a 24 hour time-span, but using that time wisely to handle a small amount of things each day.

In Chapter Nine, "A Week In The Life", you'll be able to walk through a typical week in my life, where you can see me using some of these time management methods in the context of a teen entrepreneur's day-to-day life.

Time management keeps people on track and on target, and focusing on a few things every day opens the door to classic time management "hacks" like batching.

Instead of doing three related tasks throughout the day, like making three important phone calls at 9:00am, at 1:45pm, and at 5:15pm, make them as close to one another as possible.

Batching your daily tasks allows you to perform better at the task at hand, because your mind is already primed and ready to go. Instead of having to go through the mental process to get on another phone call hours apart, you're already in the groove. Repeating yourself throughout the day exhausts you, even though you might not be able to feel it.

The concept of batching is why a lot of academic experts advise students like us to get their homework done at school! You're already thinking about the "world of academics" - it's a natural extension to just buckle down and get the work done right away.

I take a slightly different approach to this. Since I enrolled myself in a virtual academy to focus on Howdy Interactive, I get access to all of the course listings and lesson content for the entire year. Instead of doing five separate subjects per day, I do five lessons in a single subject every day.

While other students are going from class-to-class, and spending six hours a day at school, I've managed to condense the time it takes to get through my course work into about an hour per day.

This is because I already have the resources, tools, and strategies I need to work on math at the top of my head. If I had to go through the process of changing to five different subjects a day, I wouldn't be able to perform at my very best.

However, since I am just focusing on math, my brain is primed on just that. I'm able to work through the problems faster, and have the resources and things that I need to accomplish my course content at my fingertips already.

Speaking of buckling down, I talked a little bit about focusing on accomplishing less everyday. This will allow you to start thinking about accomplishing things well, instead of just checking off a to-do list.

You can start training your brain to just focusing on a few things by trying to accomplish only three things in each of your priority categories - personal, school, business sports, etc. - per day.

You might have the mental capacity to do more than three things! You are a better person than I am - I can only do a few things per day. However, If you try and cram a ridiculous amount of stuff into a single 24-hour period, you'll find yourself not giving each item the amount of attention it deserves.

A big part of my entrepreneurial philosophy is providing as much value as possible. I learned this from Walt Disney and his theme parks. I'll talk a little bit more about them in a minute, but I take attention to detail very seriously.

Only focusing on a few things per day will allow you to pay enough attention to detail for you to do a good job.

For you to have true attention to detail, that also means focusing on one thing at a time.

If you have work where you focus on doing two things at once, you'll get nothing done. Half-work is a division of your time and energy. It is perhaps the deadliest slip-up you can make, because it is the basis for procrastination.

A good example is checking your social media feed while you're working on a project. You split your attention between two things, and aren't fully engaged in what you're supposed to be getting done.

Doing less, but making sure you do it well, is the key to time management.

There might be gurus that say that you should try and pack in as much as you can in a day. And for some things, that's true! If you're making sales calls, you should make a lot of them in a single period. However, those sales calls should be one of the three things that you do for work that day.

Get what I'm trying to say?

There's no point in filling your calendar with as much shit as you can pile on there if it's not going to end up getting done. Keeping your to-do list short, but making sure you do the things on your to-do list well, will set you up for success.

Learning

A lot of teens who eventually become entrepreneurs HATE school, but love learning. This is pretty counter-intuitive, but it rings true for a lot of successful people.

What studies have found is that most entrepreneurs hate school, and don't do well in school, is because their head isn't in the right place. They're off thinking about a new project, or a new idea, or something else that's preoccupying them. If they haven't started a business yet, they might be thinking about a passion of theirs. They don't really care to listen to what the teacher has to say.

I actually know more millionaires that failed or dropped out of school than I know who passed with straight As. And it doesn't matter what their academic status was, every single one of them loved to learn about their passions. Obviously, you do too - you're reading this book right now!

The most famous and successful people in the world read every single day. Warren Buffett, Jeff Bezos, Bill Gates, you name it. The most successful people in the world are constantly learning.

But what are they learning about? They've already made it - why not quit while you're ahead?

It should be obvious - they're learning so they can expand more. Books allow people to take an idea and deliver it on a silver platter to somebody else.

It's what I'm doing right now - walking you through my ideas, my philosophies, and my methodologies on teen entrepreneurship that I've gotten from running Howdy and interviewing my colleagues. I'm helping you understand my view of this topic, something I assume you're passionate about, so you can use my information to help expand your empire.

Imagine how much more successful you'd be if Warren Buffett and Charlie Munger were your personal investment advisors!

Imagine how much healthier you'd be if you woke up and Jocko Willink was your personal trainer every morning.

Imagine the change you could make in the world if two of the greatest philanthropists of all time, Bill and Melinda Gates, held your hand in starting your non-profit.

All of this is possible! Probably not because you'll have personal access to these people, but because they've already published these ideas in the form of books, papers, blog posts, podcasts, and essays.

Getting into the success mindset requires you to think like a successful person - like a winner.

You should always be learning. It doesn't have to be about business - it could just be something that you might want to expand into at one point in the future.

As an example, I love reading about show control; the art of creating immersive experiences at theme parks around the world. I find it fascinating, and I might want to take our R&D team at Howdy in that direction.

Absorbing all of the information you can about topics that you're passionate about will set you up for success. Not only will this give you something to do, but it'll also help set into place strategies and habits that encourage that success mindset you're trying to create.

Providing Value

I have read every single inspirational book, watched every single movie, and actively listen to almost every single podcast about successful people.

Out of all of that content, I can say without a doubt, that my greatest inspiration as a teen entrepreneur is Walt Disney. He was a pioneer in the entertainment industry, and especially the work he did later in life, with Disneyland and Walt Disney World, is what makes me admire him.

Walt had an outlook on guest experience unlike anyone else in the world. He knew how to make his guests feel special, important, and a part of the story that Walt was creating.

Since his passing, many companies, both big and small, have tried to replicate that attention to guest experience. Some have gotten there, and some have failed miserably.

I strongly believe that my commitment to guest experience, and the experience of my customers, is one of the reasons that I've gotten so far as a teen entrepreneur.

I'll talk about this a little more in the sales section of this book, but people tend to buy on emotion, and then justify their purchase with logic. That means, no matter what you're selling, your job is to convince the buyer emotionally to invest in your product or service.

This is what Disney is perfect at.

Here's a good example: the Bangor State Fair, just up the street from Howdy's office, comes to town every summer. It costs about $13 for tickets, and about $7 for assorted food. If you go everyday it's open, you'll find yourself spending about 60 bucks.

I recently went to Walt Disney World, and ahead of time I purchased my tickets and dining packages all in one set. The price, for what was essentially the same product, was just over $2,700.

Why do you think this is? Both venues are providing food, rides, and entertainment, but somehow the Bangor State Fair would never be able to get away with charging $2,700 for access.

The trick is, Disney tells a better story. They work better at drawing you in emotionally, and they use your feelings to get you to purchase more and more items on your trip. With their unique stories, rides, and experience, Disney can certainly charge more because they can argue that they're providing more value.

The true mindset shift in this fourth concept of providing value is about creating win-win relationships.

A big part of scaling your business, as you will find out in the marketing and sales part of this book, is working and creating relationships with your customers, your clients, and the new set of friends you'll make embarking on a journey to financial freedom.

Instead of focusing on win-lose situations, it's a lot easier to focus on win-win situations. Not because you've suddenly grown a conscience, but because providing value to people in your life is a lot easier if you approach it from a standpoint where everyone should get something out of the relationship.

As an example, let's say that you have a brand new teacher. I run background checks on all of my high school teachers - sure, for safety reasons, but also because it helps me understand what their interests are.

Then, when it becomes Christmas time, or their birthday, or it's teacher appreciation week, I get them a small book or a small gift based on the topic they're interested in.

It's a small gesture, and it takes me about two minutes to order something on Amazon, but you immediately distance yourself in the pack by providing a win-win situation.

They get a small token of appreciation for their hard work, appreciation that they don't usually get, and now every time they see your name on an assignment, they'll remember that happy feeling that got reading through that book about fishing, or eating through that box of chocolates.

Not only does this make the teacher biased (in a good way) when grading your papers, but it also makes asking for favors, referrals, and recommendation letters a lot easier. You scratch my back, I'll scratch yours.

I like to think of money as a resource that's unlimited, because it truly is. More money is printed every single day.

The harder you work, the more money you will make. And, if you put your mind to it, you'll be able to make enough money to achieve financial freedom from a young age.

The battle is mostly about mindset - how badly do you want it?

Do you know that saying about when you're exhausted, it's a mind game, and you've only reached 40% of your physical capacity? It's exactly the same with entrepreneurship.

Self-discipline is important because the pursuit to financial freedom is full of things that you might not want to do. It's essential that you cultivate a mindset that allows you to do it anyway.

Time management will allow you to take back control of your life, and will be what will keeps you from half-assing your work. Doing fewer things better is the key to success.

Learning will allow you to continuously cultivate your mindset and set yourself up for expansion into new realms and industries. It'll also allow you to learn more about your passions, your challenges, and where you currently stand in business.

Finally, working to provide value will allow you to change the way you handle your relationships. First with your friends, family, teachers, and coaches, but as you scale your business, with your clients, vendors, and competitors.

Those four mindset points - Self Discipline, Time Management, Learning, and Providing Value, were mentioned again and again as I interviewed 25+ teen entrepreneurs for this book.

If you focus on those four things, you'll be on your way to success.

Chapter 3: Business

We've covered how to get your money right, and how to get in the headspace of a successful teen entrepreneur. Now let's talk about the fun stuff - what you picked up this book for: Business!

"Always deliver more than expected."
- Larry Page

"A big business starts small"
- Richard Branson

"Sell the problem you solve, not the product."
- Anonymous

We've finally moved on to the fun stuff! Welcome to the section where we talk about the strategies, methodologies, and principles you can use to create income through your own business.

Running a business is no small undertaking. It takes a lot of time, energy, and resources. However, the potential upside is so enormous that it makes sense for a lot of people looking to embark on this journey of financial freedom. Unlike jobs, save for commission-based positions, there is no ceiling to the amount of income you can generate, making it perfect for someone looking to increase their income as a part of the Financial Freedom Cycle.

There's plenty of advice about market research, writing business plans, finding investors, and other logistical information about starting your own business. This chapter isn't about any of that - in fact, you'll find almost none of that in this entire book.

As someone on the pursuit for financial freedom, the way you conduct business is different. This chapter talks about the methodology and principles that teen entrepreneurs are implementing around the world. It takes you through finding a kick-ass business idea, and getting started on the path to success as quickly as possible.

I don't know about you, but I don't have all the time in the world. I have school, friends, and a nice long list of shows I still need to watch on Netflix. I don't want to talk about the bureaucracy of business - I just want to sell things, make money, and go home.

Whether you're new to the big world of business, or you're already operating at six figures, I'll walk you through what has helped me and dozens of teen entrepreneurs around the world.

Make This Your Life's Work

Even if you plan to sell this company before you graduate high school or college, approaching your company like this is the only company you will ever own is super important. It puts you in the right mindset for growth.

You'll notice something as you begin to study some of the most successful people in the world: they don't move around a lot.

Jeff Bezos, at the time of writing the richest person on earth, has stayed with Amazon.com for 25 years.

Steve Jobs and Bill Gates both stayed with their company until they passed away, or decided to start a philanthropic pursuit.

Larry Page, co-founder of Google, has stayed with the company for 18 years before stepping down as CEO of Alphabet, Google's parent company.

The same thing goes for Larry Ellison, Mark Zuckerburg, Jack Dorsey, Richard Branson, Walt Disney, Elon Musk, the list goes on, and on, and on, and on.

CEOs move around a lot, from company to company, depending on who's offering the best salary, the best stock options, what company can make the most money, etc.

However, the founders of companies, those who do the hard work for the first months and years, almost always stick around until they pass away, or start a charitable organization.

That's because founders know that long-term growth trumps short term profits, or in some cases, an acquisition offer.

Your plans, deep down, don't matter. If you want to stay, that's great! If you want to sell the company and retire early, that's okay too. If you want to be chairman of the board, and retire from day-to-day activities, that's also a perfect alternative.

The goal is to treat every single day like you're going to be working on this for the rest of your life. This is your baby - so you might as well put in the extra effort to have it do as much good in the world as possible. That way of thinking will lead to increased long-term cash flow, as you put in more and more hours.

Solve A Problem

I might be getting ahead of myself, however. You might not even know how to start looking for a business idea. You don't know how to find something to do, you just know that one day, you want to have a building with your name on it, with thousands of employees reporting to you every morning.

Whatever you imagine you need to successfully start a company, you're probably mistaken.

Companies have been started without a business plan.

A website.
A staff.

An office.
Money.

None of that matters too much when you're getting started.

Your first priority, in fact your only priority when deciding what to offer, is to find a problem to solve. All companies solve problems. Every single one.

- Apple solved the lack of a personal computer.
- Whole Foods solved the lack of mainstream nutritional food.
- FedEx solved overnight shipping.
- Google solved locating websites on the World Wide Web.
- Netflix solved countless hours of boredom.

Every single company on planet earth solves a problem, and you're no different.

There's something like a bounty system on problems. People are willing to pay more to people who can solve bigger problems. Take, for example, Howdy Interactive. We solve marketing problems for companies. In exchange, they pay us about $55,000 per year to have us on retainer. However, Elon Musk is solving a variety of problems, like electric vehicles, space exploration, traffic congestion, and solar power, to name a few. He gets paid billions and billions of dollars, since those are larger problems than marketing.

Unfortunately, in most cases, there's a barrier of entry to solving larger problems. You need resources, like capital, manpower, and machinery.

As you're looking for your problem to solve, find a reasonable one based on your level of experience.

If this is your first entrepreneurial venture, then maybe pick a problem a little closer to home, like lawn mowing. Mowing someone's lawn is solving a problem! (Lawn mowing is a great industry to expand in. Labor is cheap!). So is handling food (cooking/baking), planning events, creating a magazine/publication, moving people's belongings, etc. There are plenty of business ideas you can start for no upfront capital that have a high change of success.

However, if you've been around the block a few times, try and aim for something outside of your comfort zone a little bit. Try solving a problem in a field you're not familiar with, like healthcare, agriculture, or finance. Take risks. If you have a solid stream of passive income to fund you and your project, then you can be a little bit more adventurous!

At the end of the day, depending on the problem you're solving, it will say everything you need to know regarding how you market, how you sell, who your target audience is, how much they can pay, and more.

This is perhaps the most important question you can ask yourself as you're preparing to get ready to start the process of opening your business up for customers.

Solving bigger problems is just like a bigger investment. Investing in the S&P 500 will get you a pretty average rate of return, while investing in real estate might get you further towards your investing goals, though it's riskier. It's the same thing with solving problems.

To create financial freedom, we should be concerned with getting money in the door as quickly as possible so it can start working for you with the Financial Freedom Cycle.

For that to happen as quickly as possible, it's best to, at the start, focus on solving a smaller problem instead of a larger one. You can certainly pivot to a larger problem once you have a passive income flow, but it's less-risk to get started on a smaller problem.

In fact, if you're looking for a problem to solve, try narrowing your target audience to just one person: You!

Write To One Person

Every single marketer has someone who they idol in the marketing world above everyone else. For most people, it's a very famous, life-changing marketer, like Halbert, Ogilvy, or Hemingway.
In my case, it's a guy from Evansville, Indiana. His name is Cole Schafer, and he runs a small writing shop called Honey Copy.

The reason I love Cole and his work is because he gives away so much content for free. Included in that heap of marketing goodies are his marketing rules, one of which is to, "Write to one person".

Ideally, that person should be you. You'll have a better chance of success if the problem you try and solve is one you experience on a daily basis.

There's no better way to make sure your product or service has all of its bases covered than to be someone who can test your product in real-time to see if it solves your problem.

You're familiar with this problem - you live with it every single day. You instinctively know what features your product or service needs to have because this problem affects you personally.

Solving a problem you're not familiar with is harder than one you're around every day. There may be unexpected obstacles or roadblocks that you couldn't have anticipated due to your unfamiliarity with the issue at hand.

37signals, the company behind the award-winning software Basecamp.com, has a term for this - they call it "Scratching your own itch". Their story is a perfect example of this.

37signals used to be a web design firm that had trouble collaborating on projects. They built the first version of Basecamp.com for internal use - scratching their own itch - and as more and more of their clients and vendors saw what they were working on, they said "I need to have that, too!"

Now, Basecamp.com has 3 million users - Howdy is one of 'em - all who happily pay for the service because of their approach to project management - all from finding, analyzing, and solving a problem they had to deal with on a day-to-day basis.

Who do you sell to?

The smaller you can get your target audience, the easier it is to establish dominance in your industry. You can always expand outward, but always start with a small demographic and go from there.

As an example, let's say you go into business as a videographer. At first glance, it might make good business sense to check as many boxes on your business card as possible. You advertise that you can do event videography, wedding videography, product commercials, small business commercials, and custom projects.

This does make a shred of sense - why limit yourself? The more stuff you can do, the larger your target market. Why only focus on say, product commercials, when you can do everything?

Let me ask you this - imagine a company has been working hard on their product for years. They've gone through rigorous R&D, product development, and lots of testing. Who are they going to trust to make their product commercial - someone who claims they can do everything with a camera, or someone who just does product commercials?

Why focus on capturing less than 1% of a broad market when you can easily corner 10% of a niche industry? Then, when you have enough money, clients, and referrals, expand outward.

This is actually how Howdy Interactive got its start. We started as an event marketing company, EXPOAid. Eventually, our clients had other needs, so we turned into Howdy Interactive and started with the three pillars of marketing - physical marketing, digital marketing, and experiential (events) marketing.

We started in a small subsection of the marketing niche, and grew from there to where we are today. Personally, I started in events marketing because it was a passion of mine - I loved seeing how large shows came together. A word of warning against doing things on pure passion, though - passion isn't everything.

This is a bit of a punch in the gut, but I am tasked with bringing you the reality of the situation.

If you have a passion for making sandwiches, opening a sandwich shop in Bangor, my home town, will all but guarantee disaster. On Broadway, one of our busiest streets, there are 5 sandwich shops in a .2 mile radius - more as you expand from there.

Just because you have a passion for something, doesn't mean the market is ready to meet you. It may be oversaturated, or people may just be plain not interested.

Have you overheard your classmates and friends saying things like, "I'm amazing at this, I should open a business!"? How much closer are they to opening their business than you, who is looking for a legitimate problem to solve?

You can certainly find problems to solve with something that you're passionate about - if you can do that, more power to you! It's just important to recognize that it takes more than passion to start a business.

However, if you find a problem to solve and you're passionate about it, the saying is true - you might not feel like you're actually working. Because you're passionate about the problem, you'll be more driven to create a solution.

This is the main way that large problems are solved. Elon Musk sold PayPal because he wanted to springboard into a passion of his - space exploration. That's how we got SpaceX.

If you want to just start a normal business solving a problem that's already on the market, that's fantastic! This is what I recommend 99% of the time. There's plenty of opportunity there, and hopefully the advice in this book gets you closer there.

However, there's the 1% of you that will say something along the lines of "Fuck you Nathan, stop cramping my style! If I want to change the world, I'll change the goddamn world."

Alright, I understand. For those people, I would not be doing my job as an author talking about students and business if I didn't talk about the magic of innovation, and more importantly, one college dropout that was perhaps one of the most influential innovators that the world has ever seen.

Innovation

Steve Jobs was a powerhouse. He was responsible for the design and production of so much technology that has profoundly changed the way we interact and do business.

When you create something brand new for the first time, you feel invincible - like you're on top of the world.

I felt exactly the same way when a passion-project, a hobby of mine, the world's first industry-compliant automated debt collection software, entered into release. It reduced the human labor cost by 95% in collecting on delinquent payments.

I had never been more proud of something, ever. That was the closest I ever felt to Steve, whose products earned him multiple standing ovations as he walked into a room, whether it was on stage at WWDC, or just showing off new technology at a shareholders meeting.

If all you're looking for is something as simple as money, influence, or power, you can accomplish that with any successful business, Howdy Interactive included. There's nothing too special about what we do - we provide marketing services to businesses around the United States. The business model at Howdy won't change the world. We're there to provide a service, and we're damn good at it.

However, if you want to feel acknowledged and validated on a global scale - if your main goal is to be admired by your supporters and feared by your competitors, that requires you to solve a problem in a way that nobody else has ever done before.

Steve did it multiple times - mainstreaming the personal computer, introducing the concept of holding 1,000 songs in your pocket, and creating the world's first touchscreen products.

This path of solving a problem takes a lot of work. It's a lot of trial and error, and I don't know nearly enough about it to comment further.

I'm fine with money in my bank account - I personally don't need the validation that creating a life-changing solution to a problem needs.

I know that some people do, so that's why I'm bringing this up. If you want to spend the extra time, money, and resources to innovate, go ahead! Only good things can come out of it - either you gain experience, or you have a hit product on your hands.

At the end of the day, the goal is to make as much money as quickly as possible so we can kickstart the Financial Freedom Cycle to start earning you passive income. If you can innovate and create a truly ground-breaking product in that span of time, then congratulations!

However, most of us are stuck dealing with smaller problems. No matter what problem you start working on, it's important that you start working.

Launch Quickly

The fastest way to start making money is by starting to make something. Start solving your problem.

Unless you're building something ridiculously complicated to solve a ridiculously complicated problem, there's no reason you can't have a version of your product/service that can charge people for in a week or less.

There's not a lot of planning that should go into lawn mowing, or marketing, or writing a blog, or painting, or delivering food, etc.

Just get started.

The main way you're going to grow your business, at least to start, is through your personal network. Paul Graham famously told startup founders to "do things that don't scale".

The founders of Stripe.com physically signed people up on the spot for their service when people expressed interest. A friend of mine, who does dog walking, is always carrying a Square magstripe card reader so he can take orders immediately instead of waiting for the client to pay online.

Start making something, start selling it, start taking payments. Invest half the money, and then use the rest to fuel more growth. More ads, more product, more inventory, so on and so forth.

Perfecting your idea is a waste of time - ideas are plentiful, and are only half the equation. What really matters is how you execute, and you executing depends on you starting.

It's not going to be perfect the first time around, and it's fantastic because since you're a teen, people will be more forgiving. They'll care more about the fact that young people are taking control of their lives, how noble you are, how great it is to run a business, etc.

Take this time to work out the kinks of your product or service, and then you can ramp up the amount of people you work with. You shouldn't wait to launch because you should be launching over and over again. Tweak the product, tweak your service, and launch a new, revised version tomorrow.

When a car enters production at the beginning of the year, the work doesn't stop at the R&D

department. Using user feedback, crash statistics, analytics, sales stats, and with any leftover budget, they make changes to the car every single day when it's on the line.

They aim to improve not only the safety features, but functionality that allows them to drive up the price.

At the end of the year, even though it's the same brand of car, the January 2020 car is vastly inferior to the December 2020 model.

Your product and/or service should be continuously refined throughout its lifespan. We add more value to our monthly retainer package for Howdy Interactive almost on a weekly basis, with more tools, resources, strategy calls, and content for our clients to absorb.

You shouldn't wait for the "perfect time" to launch. Just launch, and then launch again when you have an update.

I have one other piece of advice on launching products: Don't ever launch a product or a service on Friday. I can tell you what's going to happen.

You're going to launch, and get pats on the back from your friends and family who will eagerly go look at your website or buy your product.

Then, later that night, you'll get your first bug report. Something isn't working. Something's wrong with your website, or your order page, or there's an issue with the Facebook page, or you've double-booked.

You think, "That's not a problem - I'll fix it before I head home!"

As you fix that one, another one comes in. And then another one. And then another one. And so on and so forth.

The next thing you know, it's 3:00am on Monday morning, and you've been fixing problems all weekend - school starts in five hours, and you haven't slept a wink.

This is actually why I despise most events and have vowed never to host one of my own events on a full weekend.

Imagine this: I work all week, have to go work an event we were hired for on Saturday and Sunday, and then go back to work on Monday with no break. That is now a 12 day week.

We obviously still accept the contract, because it's normally worth a fair bit of money, but it still doesn't make it any less aggravating.

Never launch at the end of the week.

What you should do instead is have you and your team (if you have one) take the Friday before launch day off, and have a three day weekend.

Then, come back nice and refreshed on Monday and pull the trigger to launch. That way, when you run into bugs, you have the whole week to get things together and you don't ruin your upcoming weekend.

Upsells, Downsells, & Cross-sells

I go into every new business opportunity thinking about ways that I can provide value to my customers and make money at the same time. A great way that I handle this situation is chopping up the value into a few pieces, and using them as up, cross, and down-sells when somebody is interested in purchasing a product from Howdy.

How many products do you sell? Do you specialize in providing a specific product or service?

It turns out that if you only sell a single product or service, you're missing out on as much as up to 85% of revenue from individuals who aren't specifically in the market for that specific product or service.

Out of the billions of people on this earth, only a fraction of them are in the market for whatever you're selling. You can increase that fraction exponentially by offering multiple products, or a variation of a product, through upsells, cross-sells, and down-sells.

What we do at Howdy is we have our Kickstart Marketing Course, that helps small business owners in Maine handle their marketing. It's $3.00/mo - it's an online course that took us like a day to make.

On the confirmation page, we have a one-click-upsell where for $495/mo, we'll monitor 12+ sites like HARO (helpareporter.com) and forward relevant media opportunities to them so they can have the chance to earn some nation-wide press.

Out of the people who opt-in to get the Kickstart Marketing Course for $3.00/mo, about 1.3% get the PR Monitoring service.

Finally, out of the people who get the PR Monitoring service, we start them on a seperate marketing path - custom gifts, in-person visits, and other personalized marketing, with the attempt to earn their business for a full marketing contract (average contract value is $55,000/yr).

This is a great example of a two step upsell. But what if the small business doesn't have enough money to hire a full-time marketing firm?

We immediately down-sell them. For small businesses, we have a part-time marketing package, where small businesses get a set amount of marketing hours they can use for the month by hiring our guys. This costs about $25,000/yr, and is much more affordable for small businesses than the full-time, all-you-can-eat marketing.

But what if they're not looking for help with their marketing at all? What if all along, it turns out that sales was their issue?

Well, we don't have a sales training course, but what we do have is an affiliate account with Grant Cardone, the world's number one sales trainer.

If it turns out that sales are the issue, we recommend products based on their needs, and receive a cut of the money in exchange for our time. This is called cross-selling.

The more products and services you offer, and the more you offer during a transaction (like the one-click-upsell), the more people you'll appeal to , and the more money you'll eventually make.

The only concern is not to sell something that's wildly out-of-whack with the rest of your business. You shouldn't be selling accounting services and dog bowls under the same roof.

Done correctly, offering more products at the right time will encourage your customer to either add more on to their order, or to order a more expensive item entirely.

Take Payments. No Exceptions.

The morale of the Up/Cross/Downsell section was to break down as many barriers as possible between you and the wallets of the billions of people walking this earth.

However, wallets come in a lot of different shapes and sizes. You'd be surprised how many people still pay for items using checks nowadays, even at grocery stores. Some customers have cash, some have debit/credit cards, some have checks, and then some have virtual wallets: PayPal, WePay, Bitcoin, Apple/Samsung/Amazon/Google Pay, Venmo, Cash App, etc. Invest in the infrastructure that allows you to take payments from anyone and everyone, with no exceptions.

Take credit/debit card payments by investing in a Square account. They give you a free Square reader, and you can get a bigger one to accept Apple Pay. Get merchant accounts on all of the popular payment services. Bookmark your payment links on these services, and have a note on your phone with your accounts.

Be available for people to give you money. No excuses.

Public Perception

The reason that I'm trying to drill in the fact that you need to launch as quickly as possible is because in most cases, you are racing against public perception.

I don't know if you remember this video, but a few years ago, The New York Times published a short clip of a courtroom deposition. It's called Verbatim: What Is A Photocopier, and it walks through a deposition where an office worker doesn't know what the term "photocopier" is - it turns out everyone in the office called them a "xerox".

The moral of this short story is that the first person to market becomes the overarching leader.

Just think about Uber. Uber was founded in 2009 (its closest competitor, Lyft, was founded in 2012). Lyft vets its drivers better, its prices are cheaper, and it operates in places that Uber doesn't. (Full disclosure - I'm an Uber Platinum member)

However, what do you think of when you rideshare? What verb do you use?

You don't say, "We'll just Lyft there". You say, "We'll just Uber there!"

They were the first, and they won the battle of mental monopoly (some people call it the Google effect) and obliterated the competition so they're the only name that comes to mind when your prospects are looking for your products and services.

You probably know these pieces of trivia because they tell them to you in high school, but no adult, less no successful adult, knows or cares about who the second president or the second person who walked on the moon was. George Washington and

Neil Armstrong achieved the mental monopoly because they were the first ones to do something.

If possible, if you have a real solution to a problem, you should put it out sooner than later. Don't let your obsession with putting out the best product possible inhibit you from putting out your product first; try to achieve that mental monopoly.

If you're entering a very saturated industry, like a blue-collar service (lawn-mowing, plumbing, IT, contractor, etc.), or your own vision of a SaaS (software-as-a-service) app, then chances are you can't achieve a mental monopoly. You're not the first, but it's illogical that you can't have success.

It's time for another one of my Netflix recommendations - who here knows the story of the sad horsie? Bojack Horseman is a fantastic piece of TV that is severely underrated. There's a scene in one of the episodes that really resonates with the point of this section:

"We're number two, and that means we try harder!" - Latin Kings Gang Leader

I won't spoil any of the show. It's a fantastic watch, but let's get back to the matter at hand.

There are plenty of email services, plenty of marketing agencies, and plenty of car dealerships in a specific demographic and they do just fine. The key to gaining ground on your competitors in a crowded market is to take a drastically different approach to your problem's solution, whether that is the functionality of the solution, or the marketing surrounding it.

You should focus on outsmarting the leader, because they have more-or-less every single other advantage: more market share, more capital, more manpower, bigger lawyers, taller skyscrapers, you get the idea.

The only thing you have against them is a fresh take on the market.

A good example is Wendy's (the 8th biggest restaurant chain in the US) v. Chick-Fil-A (the 21st biggest). These are calculated by locations in the United States.

I love both restaurants, but let's not kid ourselves about what comes to mind when we think about traditional fast food: it's a greasy, unhealthy, only-stop-there-if-you-have-to kind of food.

Both are technically fast food restaurants, but Wendy's came with the preconceived notion of exactly what a fast food restaurant would look like.

Chick-Fil-A, on the other hand, took a completely different route than any of the big brands - McDonald's, Burger King, or Wendy's.

They prioritized healthy cooking and customer service, and as a result charged a little bit higher than something you'll find at one of the three big fast food stops.

Chick-Fil-A was quite behind on the list of "biggest restaurants", so they flipped the conceptualization of what exactly a "fast food restaurant" was on its head, and came up with an entirely new concept; an alternative.

Now, arguably, Chick-Fil-A has more die-hard fans than Wendy's, McDonald's, or Burger King does - possibly even combined.

Unless you're pioneering a new industry, there will always be some overlap between what you're doing and another company. Taking an entirely different approach will cause customers to look at you like as a helpful alternative, not as just another knock-off. Inevitably, as you grow, people will want to help you improve your product or service. They'll give you feedback, either verbally or through a review.

Whether this is solicited or not, appreciate it all the same. Read through it, make sure you understand their concerns, respond if necessary, and then throw it in the trash.

Customer Feedback

You shouldn't be keeping track of customer feedback. It overcomplicates things, and I want to make this process as easy as possible for you. This is one less thing to worry about.

When the collective of your audience, meaning the majority, not just one person, want a change in your offering, they'll let you know. They won't shut up about it - it's the only thing you'll be able to hear until you fix it or developer it.

Use real, live humans as your indicator as to what features are wanted and what you should work on next. Chances are, they've already told you - you're just not listening.

I guarantee you none of your customers have ever woken up in the morning and said, "Gee, if only [your] product was delivered a little bit slower, then I'd be all set!". I can also guarantee you they've never said, "Wow, I sure wish [they] don't ever make this product cheaper!".

When it comes time to tweak your offering and put out a second version, focus on the things that can't change.

In the grand scheme of things, the marketing outlook on social media has changed dozens of times. First, it was Facebook, then Twitter, then Linkedin for B2B businesses, and now TikTok is the big one. The way to sell your products online has changed dozens of times. First we had sole websites, then peer-to-peer marketplace sites like Ebay, then conglomerates like Amazon.com and Walmart, and now sales funnels are starting to become very popular.

All of these options, both for marketing and selling, have pros and cons. However, the things you should be focusing on are permanent features - things that as they change, only have pros.

Take Amazon.com for example. They started with very slow shipping. They realized this was a pain point for their customers, so they introduced Amazon Prime, which offered unlimited two-day shipping. Just this year, they announced that Amazon Prime would be switching to one-day shipping. Amazon's commitment to solving this particular problem is because of the first quote - nobody is going to wake up and say "I wish my Amazon package could come a little bit slower," - that's never going to change, so that's what they're focusing on.

Be on the lookout for occasions that you're spending too much time perfecting things that don't matter too much, like the shade of green on your website footer, or what social media platform you use.

Focus on perfecting your product by talking to customers and predicting what they'll never want changed, but make sure you differentiate between what feedback is in line with what you're building, and what feedback isn't great. Everyone should have some set of values or opinions they want to instill with their product or service.

Take A Side!

Making an opinionated product will help you get a cult following for what you're selling. A good example of this is this book. I push a lifestyle of total commitment to financial freedom - it's not for everyone. If you're more into having things grow naturally and slowly, I'd recommend the book REWORK by Jason Fried and David Heinemeier Hansson.

However, if you're into the style of aggressive expansion, and committing to things 110%, this book is perfect for you.

People aren't just looking for features in a solution - they're looking for an approach. They're looking for a vision. And the only way you're going to successfully achieve a vision is by taking a stance. The stance may be one that a lot of people like, or one that some people might not agree with.

An example is Alina Morse - a teen entrepreneur, and the youngest person to ever be featured on the cover of Entrepreneur magazine.

She founded a company called Zollipops, and she develops a line of sugar-free candy products. Her company takes a very firm stance against candy that hurts your teeth. She incorporates this into all of her marketing materials, and she frequently does media interviews about this stance - it's the hill she's prepared to die on.

If she was just selling another brand of lollipop, chances are nobody would give a damn. But because she took a stance against harmful candy, she's used that to her advantage to build a base of loyal customers and fans. The stance you take doesn't need to be one that splits America in half, like political parties. It can be something as broad as taking a stance against candy that hurts your teeth.

However, the sooner you can show people that you're taking a stance, the sooner they'll have more context about the values of your company. Now, more than ever, consumers care about the ethics, morality, and values of the companies they're doing business with.

Blizzard, in October of 2019, supported mainland China in the Hong Kong protests, and people flipped out - many people deleted their accounts, asked for refunds, and planned to storm Blizzcon (their annual event).

Unfortunately, in this scenario, it was a bit of a lose-lose because they were trying to make two sides happy: the Chinese government, and American consumers. Picking the correct side and building an opinionated product or service can be the difference between average & intense growth.

Quick Wins

To conclude this chapter, I wanted to talk about the concept of quick wins and positive reinforcement. Focus on achieving a set of smaller wins on a more frequent scale than larger wins periodically.

The human brain relies on positive praise and feedback to function correctly. Going too long without positive reinforcement (i.e., a win), is not good for your morale, and may lead to burnout and abandonment of your project, and subsequently your journey to financial freedom.

The longer something takes, the less likely you're going to finish it. You have millions of things going on - academics, friends, relationships, business, family, chores, etc.

Focusing on sets of quick wins will keep the project at the forefront of your mind for a longer period of time, which will allow you to get things done.

Chapter 4: Marketing

Marketing is an essential part of your business. Inbound leads are the easiest to sell your product and service to, as they're qualified and predisposed to hand you a check.

"You can't sell anything if you can't tell anything."
- Beth Comstock

"Stopping advertising to save money is like stopping your watch to save time." - Henry Ford

"The best marketing doesn't feel like marketing"
- Tom Fishburne

Marketing is perhaps one of the easiest things to get wrong, and the hardest things to get right. Getting people to hand you money on auto-pilot is every business owner's dream. Having a stream of qualified people who are ready to buy your product when they walk through the door is a great way to turn your business into a form of passive income.

This is one of my areas of expertise because of my marketing firm, Howdy Interactive. I built it from the ground up using these techniques, tips, and tricks. Howdy Interactive's worked alongside NBC, Amazon, Five Guys, Eventbrite, and a few other big names - I guess what we do works.

What I've found is when a lot of people, like teen entrepreneurs, are new to marketing, they just copy what everyone else is doing because they have no idea where to start, or worse, treat marketing as an afterthought. This is a very dangerous way to approach marketing, and can immediately ruin your credibility.

Targeted Marketing

The goal of marketing is to put your message in front of the people who are best qualified to receive it. In your case, it's putting your product or service in front of your target audience. If you own a landscaping company in Omaha, it makes no sense targeting all 230 million American Facebook users when you can narrow that down to people who have a direct need for your service. It's like trying to throw a dart at a bull's-eye while you're wearing a blindfold. Your chance of hitting the bull's-eye is almost impossible, but this is how a lot of people new to the business scene approach marketing.

However, when you take the time to select the prospects that you market to, you suddenly become desirable because your solution can kick the shit out of their problems. It's a common misconception that you want to reach as many people as possible in marketing - you just want to reach those desperately need what you have.

Imagine all of the soda in the world evaporated overnight, and you were the only person left with a closet full of Coca-Cola. Even if you can't market for the life of you, or you're not a great salesperson, you could still sell out of the Coca-Cola because you're the only one who has any left.

One of the world's greatest copywriters, Gary Halbert, often asked his audience, "If you were going to open a restaurant, and you could choose just one advantage to improve your restaurant's chance of success, what would it be? Great food? A clean design? Fast service? Friendly staff?" Gary said, "The best advantage you could have would be a starving crowd right outside your door."

If you can determine who your target market is, usually an extension of the problem your business is trying to solve, then you just made your marketing 10 times easier. Remember, most people focus on developing a great product and then worry afterwards about who might buy it. That's when they start marketing, as an afterthought.

If you can find your target market first by finding a problem to solve, you can start implementing marketing strategies that are much easier than wasting time trying to attract as many people as possible.

Joe Polish, marketing juggernaut and one of the most connected people I know, says that you must have three things to sell something. You must have a product or service, you must have a sales/marketing message, and you must have a delivery system. He says that most people either think about their product, or their delivery system, but think very little about developing an effective marketing message. He's right.

The majority of new business owners, and especially people who don't know what they're doing (like teens!) focus on "new and exciting!" marketing techniques when they fail at something. If email doesn't work for them, they try social media with very little success. Then they move on to email marketing, posters, SMS, one after another as they don't see results. The reason they're not seeing results isn't because they're using the incorrect marketing tool - it's because they're not developing an effective marketing message.

Image Advertising v. Education-Based Marketing

The large majority of advertising today is called "Image Advertising" - it focuses on the product/service being promoted, or the company behind it. The thought is that if you see a picture of some company's office, or a video of their product, or a discount code for your first purchase, all of the sudden you'll want to buy it.

This can work in very limited instances, none of which apply to you. For example, if you are an established brand, like Coca-Cola, then this is where most of your money should go. Establishing brand awareness and continuing to keep an omnipresence-like state in advertising is important if everyone knows who you are. Coca-Cola has an advertising budget of billions of dollars, and a team of hundreds that work on marketing campaigns year-round. Starting out, you might have some money, and you might have a small team of friends, employees, and family. You don't have the resources to pull of a brand awareness campaign yet.

In your case, your messaging - not the medium or the delivery system of the messaging - is what's important about your marketing efforts. Just think about it: when you go on Youtube, what are you more likely to watch casually? An established creator who puts hours of work into each video, that obviously shows thought and care, or some new creator who's creating seven new videos a day, just trying to churn them out? Obviously, you're going to go with the more established creator.

Both of those videos are delivered through Youtube. That part doesn't change at all. The only thing that changed your decision - that tilted your preference one way or the other - was content was on the other side of the thumbnail.

One of the things I preach, heavily, at Howdy Interactive is the importance of education-based marketing. The easiest, cheapest, and fastest way to get new clients is by providing value upfront. A good example is this book! Don't worry, you're not the target audience. You can sit back and suck as much value out of here as you can. But for schools, conferences, and companies who want to hire me as a speaker, or hire me to consult, this book is a piece of education-based marketing that I can use to show that I know what I'm talking about.

If you can provide upfront value to your target audience, not just blast out a boring advertisement, you'll notice your marketing working better than everyone else. When you do something for free, people will feel committed to do something for you in return. Who would you rather buy from - a company that's only there to sell a product, or a company that goes out of their way to educate you about their products and services, and ways you can use their solution to help your life? The answer is obvious.

Ways To Create Educational-Based Marketing Content

Luckily, there are many ways that you can create educational content for your marketing. With the internet, it's literally easier than ever to start implementing these strategies for free. Look at all of the examples! Books, DVDs, articles, podcasts, etc. People don't make these out of the goodness of their hearts, they make them so they can upsell you on relevant products and services.

One of the most common tools is an industry guide. Joe Polish calls these "consumer reports", Shaun Buck calls them "Newsletters"... - the point is, it doesn't matter what you call them. They work.

An industry guide is a collection of articles, testimonials, walk-throughs, and information about your products, services, and industry. Howdy Interactive publishes one called "Marketing In Maine" - a complete guide to businesses who want to increase their revenue and profits in Maine through personalized marketing. It has articles such as "The Only Way To Revive Dead Leads (One Guy Made $180M!)", "Marketing In-House v. Retaining An Agency", and "How To Make Your Advertising up to 500% More Effective!", all of which were based on research, statistics, and publicly available information on Maine and the best ways to advertise here.

I put a copy on my website, and sent a link out to people I knew who were having trouble with marketing. It worked wonders - in the first month, I had three new marketing clients, and to this day, that industry guide has opened the door to hundreds of thousands of dollars worth of opportunities for me.

Creating video content is also another valuable advertising tool. Remember I was talking about our cheap Kickstart Marketing Course in chapter 3? Just like this book allows me to sell some companies on speaking/consulting gigs, the Kickstart Marketing Course allowed us to sell some companies on our fully-fledged retainer program.

The Kickstart Marketing Course was a value-provider if I'd ever seen one - 12 marketing strategies, delivered once a month, that we've used at Howdy for our corporate clients. It paved the way for the conversation about bringing on some of the KMC students for our high-ticket package that otherwise wouldn't have been able to happen.

If you don't want to go through putting together an entire video program, or an industry guide, try experimenting with just a single blog post on a specific topic. These can be written in a few hours, and you can post them on a variety of places, like your website, content aggregators, and third party blogging sites (like Medium.com).

I've written blog posts on pricing psychology, guest experience, and marketing, but you can tailor your blog posts to the type of business you run. If you make granola bars, try writing about how you source ingredients, or a behind-the-scenes look at how you make and distribute them. If you do landscaping, a story about best practices to keep your garden flourishing would help you establish that you know what you're talking about.

No matter what you eventually decide, each of these pieces of education-based marketing have one thing in common - they're all examples of auto-pilot advertising. They're online 24 hours a day, and allow you to speak to, educate, and sell to clients without manual effort. Furthermore, these tools (because they're valuable content), rank high for search engine optimization. When people Google a specific question in your industry, your new marketing tools have a chance of ranking high.

Market Like A Person, Not Like A Company

As a teen entrepreneur, the odds are stacked against you by default. This is something the global young entrepreneur movement is trying to change.

However, you have one advantage that nobody can take away from you at the beginning: your size.

You're most likely starting out as a one-person shop, maybe two or three people max. You are a small team, one that is agile and ready to pounce.

You're not brought down by corporate intake forms, or company-wide policies, or even better than all of this: the stupid, foolish way that most companies deal with their marketing today.

You might think that because you're small, and lack the experience of the bigwigs, that you need to make up for it in your marketing efforts by acting very formal and professional, kind of like a big company. That's bullshit. Knock it off.

Marketing like a person, instead of marketing like a corporation generates better results and engagements, no matter the target audience.

We're seeing the endless formality/monotony less and less with the 21st century brands who are trying to appeal to a younger

generation, but what about companies who do something normal, like sell water pumps?

I'm going to take the liberty of showing you a traditional, 135-employee accounting company who published this honest-to-god tweet on their profile:

> Before any contract is awarded,
> #DCAA auditors will examine your
> company's accounting system to
> validate that it is capable of
> maintaining records according to
> DCAA standards. #govcon
> #governmentcontractor
> #outsourcedaccounting

What the *fuck* was that?

Even if you're in the accounting/government purchasing industry, that reads like somebody is being forced to write that at gunpoint. (By the way, if that was your tweet, email me so I can kick your marketing team into shape please! ns@nathan-sykes.com)

When you're agile, small, casual, and most importantly run by teen entrepreneurs, you have a unique ability to connect with individuals in a way that large corporations can't.

I could have chosen any corporation and would have gotten the exact same result, with maybe a little less legalese (because of the government contracting).

Let's look at an example with a brand that actively tries to market itself as a person - here are one of their tweets:

> Our holiday sets are officially here. Choose between our limited-edition Winter Winston handle or our classic Truman. Both complete with all the makings of a handsome shave—in a shiny gift box fit for the season.

Now obviously you need to cut the first brand a *little* slack, it's hard to compare accounting to razors, but even still.

The difference that making yourself sound like a human caused was extraordinary, just because of the way they worded a 280 character social media post. (It goes without saying that the second tweet about the shaving company received a ton of more engagements).

The Point Of Creating Content

The key to selling large amounts of anything - coffee mugs, marketing services, plush animals, etc. - is building up an audience. The only realistic way to do that is to provide content, and to reel people in using valuable information.

There's nobody that's been more influential in getting this book made than Tucker Max. I've been following along with his resources at Scribe Media, and I had the opportunity to meet him at Genius Network a while back.

He's a fucking awesome, down-to-earth, guy. He went on Tim Ferriss's podcast talking about how he promoted his book and got on the New York Times Bestseller list, and shared some tips about building an audience. I think they were somewhat helpful:

- Give Your Content Away For Free, And Keep It Free

- Make Your Content Easily Shareable

- Promote Your Content In Places That Make Sense, But DO NOT Spam

- Build Relationships With People Who Can Help You, And Vice Versa

- Engage Your Fans, But Only In The Ways That Are Authentic & Provide Value

- Everything You've Read About Effective Marketing Doesn't Matter... Unless You Have Content People Like.

Alright, that's all I'm stealing from him, I promise. I'm going to deep-dive into this points on my own, using examples from my life and the lives of fellow teen entrepreneurs.

I publish a podcast and a blog post at least three times a week. They're all up and available for viewing at nathan-sykes.com, if you're interested in looking at them.

Mostly, it's rambling about how teen entrepreneurs should handle a specific issue (at the time of writing, today's episode was about reducing school-load and whether you should drop out).

I would never think about charging for it, because it's one of the best forms of marketing for me - the moment I put it behind bars, 85% of my marketing effort has vanished.

You'll also notice that I publish both a podcast and a blog post, not just one or the other.

However, they're about the same issue. Why do I do this? I do it to make the content easily shareable. Some people prefer listening to podcasts, some people just want to skim through what I have to say and move on. Both of these methods can easily be shared by just copying the URL of the post.

I interview a lot of people in this book - a lot of very high-performing, successful high school/college students that are changing the world.

I've only met three of them in-person, and I wouldn't consider myself good friends with any of them, just friendly acquaintances (this isn't meant to be offensive, we just don't know each other that well).

However, I still picked them to be featured in my book because they're big names in the world of teen entrepreneurship, and I hope to build a relationship with them.

In exchange for being featured in one of the most comprehensive books on teen entrepreneurship published to date, I hope they'll be proud of that fact and will let their followers and clients know about the book.

It's a mutually beneficial proposal, and I can build on to our relationship from there.

You'll notice I don't actively have an email list. I don't believe in them, specifically for my scenario. I publish a blog post that could easily be content for an email list, but sending an email every single day is what I consider spam. I do have a Twitter page though, and I actively post/retweet content I think can be valuable to my followers.

I focus on quality v. quantity in the conversations I have with my audience, because their time is valuable and wasting it with stupid bullshit is a great way for me not to have an audience anymore.

And finally, I certainly think that my content is valuable and interesting, but that ultimately lies with you, the consumer.

If you have read this far, you probably think my book is interesting - thank you!

Referrals

While using education-based marketing is easy to get new clients who have never heard of you or your business, it's even easier to get clients by asking your existing customers to refer people. Referrals are one of the best ways to acquire new customers. The cost of acquisition is significantly lower, and the new prospect you're talking with may be more pre-disposed to buy whatever you're selling because someone they trust referred them to you.

Earning referrals means you need to be referral-worthy. If you're going to take advantage of opportunities like referrals, you need to run your business where your customers would have no problem referring new clients. If you normally do sketchy things, or worse, make your clients feel unwelcome, they won't be motivated to do business with you in the future, and furthermore, they won't be motivated to send new clients your way.

If you do a good enough job, many clients will happily refer new customers to you anyway, if you just ask. However, it's a lot easier to convince them to do so if you're offering some kind of reward. That's actually how I marketed this book! I offered free rewards to people who got their friends, colleagues, and family to sign up for my mailing list. At Howdy Interactive, we pay $3,000 to anyone who refers the new company to join our corporate marketing retainer program.

Just asking my existing base of clients and fans for new customers has given me tens of thousands of dollars of opportunity in the last month alone. It's a form of marketing that has no monetary cost to you, and can help strengthen the relationship between you and your existing clients.

Testimonials

However, some of your clients might not know anybody who's in the market for your product or service. That's perfectly fine! In that case, what you should do is gather social proof in the form of testimonials. Testimonials are important because they provide the proof to people who have no idea who you are that you're a legitimate, reputable business. I ask every single one of my clients for a testimonial, and I'm even going to ask you at the end of the book to give me your honest review.

When you're soliciting testimonials, it's important to get them from everyone - even people who you think wouldn't give you a five star rating. You don't need to display those, but it's important that you get that feedback so you know what to do better in the future.

A written testimonial accompanied by a headshot is perfectly fine, but the best way for a testimonial to be portrayed is through a video. You can feel the emotion and connection that a client has with your business a lot better. We've found that casual selfie videos perform best.

When you have a good number of testimonials, you can begin to sprinkle them throughout your online presence and other marketing materials. For example, you could put some in your industry guide, at the end of your videos, and sprinkle into your blog posts. If you run a business that allows people to order online, you can also put some on social media as evergreen content - content that's not time sensitive, like a "Happy Holidays!" post. It can be posted at any time of the year, in between days where you're producing your educational-based marketing strategies.

The goal of my marketing strategies, the ones here and the ones I use at Howdy Interactive, are to implement strategies that perform very well for little to no cost. You'll notice I didn't talk about social media, email, or any other digital marketing strategies. I didn't talk about paid advertising, or video production, or attending events, trade shows, and craft fairs. That's because there is so much in the world of marketing to cover that I could never fit into a small book like this. It takes a lot of time, money, and energy to learn how to market successfully using all of those different tools, and at the end of the day, you can use a variety of them to complement your education-based marketing. What I want to give you is the best format for your marketing, (education-based - not image ads!) so you can immediately start seeing results and climbing that path to financial freedom.

Don't Waste Money

A client of mine ordered $6,000 in custom polo shirts, duffel bags, and other swag to promote a health & fitness retreat he offered as a part of his health company. His thinking was that he could sell it at a premium once people got to "know his brand" a little better.

I'm sure you can imagine what happened next. I haven't been in touch with that client for a few months, but that last time I was in his office, the boxes of march were sitting in the basement of his office, untouched, more than 24 months after he ordered them.

Don't waste money on marketing shit you don't need. "Merchandise" and "swag" is at the heart of this.

Nobody cares about your brand, at least until you change the public's perception. Passing out free t-shirts and stickers is not the way to do that.

There are plenty of actionable, trackable things you can spend your money on: building an email list, Facebook ads, sales forecasting software, billboards, whatever.

Swag and other stupid bullshit (like custom fidget spinners!) are clues that you don't know how to spend your money, and you're just doing this so you can show off your business.

Let me be clear, though - a few custom t-shirts are fine! I ordered 5 t-shirts with some variation of the Howdy Interactive logo on 'em. My staff have a few a piece as well. And for very
fancy events, I have a Howdy Interactive pin I place on my lapel. Those are perfectly fine.

However, buying 1,500 Howdy Interactive t-shirts and passing them out around Bangor is not a good idea for me.

Mark Cuban is actually famous for saying this - a variation of this is one of his twelve rules of entrepreneurship. If this rule works for Mark Cuban, it can work for you!

Chapter 5: PR

PR is a great long-term marketing strategy, especially when you know how to use the appeal of being a teen entrepreneur correctly. Tons of niche and mass-media sites are looking for inspiring young people to do stories on!

"Some are born great, some achieve greatness, and some hire a PR firm." - Daniel J. Boorstin

"A good PR story is infinitely more effective than a front-page ad." - Richard Branson

"Advertising is saying you're good. PR is getting someone else to say you're good." - Jean-Louis Gassée

Every teen entrepreneur on planet earth is a walking news story. Using that fact to your advantage can land you interviews, features, and mentions in some of the most famous and relevant publications in your industry. Media companies LOVE teenagers doing cool things because it's great content that a lot of people click on.

Earned media is one of the best resources for growth because unlike most advertising, it doesn't cost any money - you earn it! An appearance in a relevant publication can propel you to new heights in terms of your authority in an industry.

Back when print media was all the rage, newspapers, magazines, and other media publications could command a higher price for advertisement. However, due to the deflation of advertising costs that accompanied the introduction of the internet, journalists don't have the time or ability to go hunting for stories, doing lots of research, and presenting a polished piece a few days later.

These days, journalists are looking for stories that come pre-packaged so they can tweak some things, meet their deadlines, and move on. That, combined with the fact that you're a teen entrepreneur, will be your biggest weapon in getting attention for yourself.

Developing A Story Angle

The first step in landing yourself in the press is to develop a story angle. It's the spin you plan to put on your business/product to make it appealable to readers. Journalists do this for a living, so they have a nose for bullshit. If you're blatantly self-promoting your products without providing value to the readers, then they'll skip over your pitch.

A story angle is not a one-time concept. Your angle should be timely, relevant, and should be updated every few months to stay relevant. For example, at the time of writing, TikTok is a major player in the world of social media. An angle about how a teen entrepreneur is using TikTok to advertise their gardening products would be a fantastic story! An angle about a new line of gardening products, complete with the Amazon link, is not - that's blatant self-promotion.

Furthermore, depending on the journalist and publication you're pitching your story to, you might need to change the way you pitch the angle. For example, if you're pitching to my city's local paper, the Bangor Daily News, you might want to make it sound like a human interest story - "Maine Teen Uses TikTok To Market Her Business"

However, if you're pitching to a publication like the Wall Street Journal, they are more focused on finances. You'll have more success pitching the angle from a finance standpoint, like "Here's How A Teenager Uses TikTok Instead Of Paid Advertising". This paints using the social media app as a tool to reduce marketing costs, which is perfect for the Wall Street Journal.

Creating a good angle is important because it clarifies what you need to say, and helps determine the audience you need to say it to. As you develop more and more story angles, make sure they're set towards a specific niche target audience.

Mass Media v. Niche Media

If you have the opportunity to get featured in a mass-media publication, like The New York Times, or The Verge, that's great!

The first time you're featured in a mass-media publication is a very exciting time - it gives you validation that you're on the right path.

However, features on The Wall Street Journal are not normal for anybody, not just teen entrepreneurs. What you should instead be searching for are niche media publications.

Being featured in mass-media is a dream that you can easily get caught chasing.

Realistically, one of the best applications you can use for mass-media coverage is putting a little blurb on your website that says "As seen in The Los Angeles Times" - the impact of mass-media publications are extremely diluted.

On the other hand, niche media, while not as "sexy" as getting a feature in The Boston Globe, can be more beneficial to your business because it places you, your company, and your message in front of your target market, and more than likely, the decision makers in your target market.

When my team and I go try to find media opportunities, we focus on pitching niche media. Since we offer marketing services, it makes no sense pitching to media that covers the marketing industry - that's not where our target market is at.

Instead, what we do, is we think about where our ideal client would look to as a source of reliable guidance for advice, inspiration, tips, and tricks.

For example, if you ran a landscaping company in Maine, a reasonable PR decision would be to try and land a feature in Maine Home & Garden or a similar publication or site.

You will certainly be helped by the fact that you're a teen entrepreneur - you're young, which means you're exciting and different, which means you have more of a possibility of being read, which means the publication makes money through advertisements.

More often than not, mass-media reporters also ask if you've been featured in any other publications, and it's a lot easier to gain credibility in the ranks of mass-media if you start out by pitching niche media. Niche media will have more of a direct impact on your business and your pursuit to financial freedom. And now, getting access to niche media reporters is easier than ever.

Utilizing HARO

Did you know that most public relations firms do less than three hours of work a day? Some of the most successful ones do, in fact.

They use a free tool (that's open to the public), that actively solicits stories from publications, both niche and mass-media, from around the world.

It's a big, big, open secret in the public relations world. It's called HARO: Help A Reporter Out.

Help A Reporter Out has been responsible for getting me quoted in/interviewed/featured on CNBC, CBS, Business Insider, FOX News, Reader's Digest, and Buzzfeed. These aren't large articles, but they allow you to put the "As featured in..." credits on your brand, both business and personal. In addition to those mass-media opportunities, I've been featured on plenty of niche sites about success, leadership, and opportunity - right were the decision makers for the companies in my target market lie.

HARO also got me in the room with HBO, where I'm currently in talks to be in a documentary show of theirs. I'm super excited, but can't share more information because then the production company would kill me.

Let me go back to the three hours a day - almost all public relation firms don't pitch stories to reporters, they wait for reporters to come to them.

Every single day, at 5:35am, 12:35pm, and 5:35pm EST, an email gets sent out to everyone on the (FREE!) HARO list.

The PR firms then sort out what opportunities would be a fit for their clients, email/call them to get a response and put together a two-sentence pitch, and send it to the reporter (along with information about their client's business) to see if they're interested.

It's so simple in fact, we offer it to our clients for free as a part of our all-you-can-eat retainer marketing firm, and it probably costs less than $600/week in labor.

It's free to sign up, for anyone, and you can start receiving stories immediately. They do offer paid plans, but that's for stuff like online viewing of the story archive and whatnot - you don't need that.

Go try it out. Seriously. I might write a whole book just about HARO. If this is the ONE PR trick you learn from this book, it's already worth whatever you paid for it just based on the free PR this tip will land you.

Seriously. Go right now. It's been going for 7 years, and has no signs of stopping. 15 emails a week with requests from publications looking to talk TO YOU FOR FREE. The only thing that HARO can get better at is getting more local reporters on their platform. Local media outlets, unfortunately, tend not to use HARO unless you're in a major metropolitan area. If you're hanging out with me in Maine, it's not every day we see a HARO request from the Bangor Daily News.

The Local Press

While HARO is great for niche media and mass media, getting local attention can, in some cases, be even better.

Local media is very easy to get to if you have a good angle, and can you help establish your media reel/kit that larger media organizations may ask for. There are plenty of stories on teen entrepreneurs - all you need to do is Google "high school entrepreneur" and you'll be met with success stories from all sorts of individuals, some of them my friends, from all sorts of news sites.

High-performing teens are a big draw, kind of like successful individuals of any type. People watch very successful people because it serves a twofold purpose - it provides a level of comfort watching other people succeed, and it helps motivate people who are looking for that extra push.

So how is it possible to get on local media without the help of HARO?

My strategy for local media is very long-term. I'll walk you through an example case.

I joined the app Nextdoor - it's a private social media network for the neighborhood. I joined this particular app because 60% of my neighborhood was on it, and I had a hunch I was living near a reporter for a popular local show.

It turns out my hunch was right! Nextdoor gave me access to a lot of information I wouldn't have known otherwise, and I went to introduce myself to her.

I began by pitching her as a source for any business/teen entrepreneur related news, which itself is rare in Bangor. She said she'd consider me, which in reporter-speak says "there's nothing available right now", and thanked me for my interest. But there was an upside here - now she knew who I was.

I sent her a follow-up email thanking her for the chat, and began developing a long-term friendship with this reporter.

It wasn't long before she interviewed me for another project, and now she is one of the most important people I know who's helping me bring this book to the attention of the local market in Maine.

When it comes to local media, they're always looking for the next big story. Prove yourself to a reporter, but don't make the relationship one-sided.

Everything should be a win-win - remember this from the mindset chapter?

Make a friend instead of focusing on grabbing a spot on the local news - you're an extraordinary person for taking the dive to become an entrepreneur - you'll get there soon enough.

A reporter receives hundreds of pitches every single day. It's up to you to make yours stand out of the crowd, and for that you have about 20 seconds.

You're already at an advantage because of your unique status as a teen entrepreneur, so take advantage of that and factor it into your pitch.

A Timely Pitch

Newsrooms are looking for something timely and controversial, to drive views. Don't pitch newsrooms with the idea that you're going to get a feature on your product or service. As I said before, that's blatant self-promotion. Pitch them on something relevant.

As an example, CBS and FOX News had just done a piece on how companies try to exploit you during free trials. We've had some trouble cancelling on free trials ourselves, so one of my media guys, Rob, got in touch with CBS and FOX News and pitched them:

"Hey, my name is Rob Parker and I have a timely pitch for you. I saw you did a story on how companies abuse their free trial program to increase their bottom line at the expense of guest experience. The company I work for is owned by a teen entrepreneur, and has a lot of trouble with free trials, and we'd love to talk with your reporters so you can get some real-life perspective for a follow-up."

Sure enough, both companies agreed. It was my first media opportunity on FOX News, and my third on CBS.

As a result of the article, we saw about 1,000 trackable engagements come in to my blog/podcast as a result of those two news stories alone.

The "Perfect Pitch" needs to be just long enough to be jam-packed full of information, but doesn't overwhelm the person on the receiving line.

It needs to be relevant and controversial - Rob's pitch was relevant to another story they did, and controversial (we're calling companies out on national media for deceptive practices!).

The biggest rule to follow when pitching a newsroom (not an individual reporter) is to make it as far from about yourself as possible. If they smell blatant self-promotion, they'll hang up on you and your reliability factor in that organization will go down. Focus on providing value, and you'll get value back.

If you have a specific event happening, and think people will actually be interested, instead of providing value in an article disguised as an advertisement, just send in a press release!

Navigating Press Releases

Press releases are great for announcements regarding your company. These shouldn't be used for human interest stories, personalized reporting, or in most cases, pitching to mass-media publications. If a press release is longer than a page or two, the engagement rate drops considerably - so it's up to you to make sure it's precise and conveys exactly what it needs to, with nothing else. This is not the time for filler.

The goal of press releases is to answer the five W questions you learned in your english class: who, what, where, when, and why. There are six parts to a kick-ass press release. Depending on your situation, industry, and announcement, you can add more, but you can't go wrong with this traditional format!

After you have your headline, you always start with a summary of what your press release is trying to achieve. This is the most important part of the entire release - most journalists just read the summaries of press releases before deciding on what stories to run with. I'm going to use an example - let's pretend that Howdy is opening a new office in Portland, in addition to our office in Bangor.

We'd start the press release by explaining who we (Howdy Interactive) are, what we're doing (building a new office) that warrants a press release, and how this is going to impact people (economic/hiring impact).

When you have your summary, you should explain the problem that consumers are facing, and the solution that your organization provides. For example, if you're starting a photography business, you might state that the problem is that Maine-based clients can't get affordable photography to commemorate their events, and you're solving that issue with a network of Maine-based photographers who can be ordered at an hour's notice.

It always helps when you give data points to a journalist. It helps cement the credibility of your story. This data doesn't need to be yours, you can just nab it offline. For example, if you created a medical brace for adults with arthritis, a good statistic to put into your press release would be "According to the CDC, 23% of all adults - over 54 million people - have arthritis."

After you include some data, a quote from you, a customer, or a credible third party (like a celebrity) will help provide additional credibility. Ideally, this quote should be related to your status as a teen entrepreneur - that is what we've found is more successful in landing stories for teen entrepreneurs. Remember, being a teen that does cool stuff is a great news story - let the journalist know that.

The call to action is the final content piece of your press release. The CTA should explain what exactly you want the reader to do. When I was sending out a press release for this book, my CTA was for people to check it out on Amazon.

Finally, the media contact is simply the contact information about who the journalist can reach out to for more questions and interview requests. More often than not, just put yourself - journalists love talking with successful teens!

When you're sending out a press release, make sure to send it as early as possible, like 5:00am-ish. If you send it towards midday, or worse, in the afternoon, the reporter is already busy writing their stories for that day - you've struck out of luck!

Refunds

To conclude this chapter, I want to tell you a guest experience-related PR tip that might help you avoid disaster in the long run. I've sold all sorts of items, ranging from boosted boards to marketing services, tech gizmos to raffle tickets. I've sold them for a variety of organizations, the most obvious suspect being my own company.

And out of the thousands of items I have sold in my life so far as a teen entrepreneur, nobody has ever asked me to refund a payment.

Until last week.

Reading his email made me realize that he didn't use the program correctly (the product in question was access to my exclusive PR program called World-Class PR).

I almost wanted to drive to his office and slap him, because it was apparent he was doing so many things wrong.

Instead, I calmed down and sent him a refund. He had his money back almost immediately.

I think it's very important, both from an ethics and a PR perspective, to always refund your client's transactions upon request. It's just the world we live in nowadays - think of it as the cost of doing business.

What if the reason they're returning it is because it's not the right product for them, not because it's a piece of shit?

Imagine if they have a friend looking for a similar item! If you don't struggle when they ask for a refund, you'll keep the door open for them to refer more customers and clients your way if they're looking for something more suited to what you do.

However, if you decide to slam the door and keep the money, sure, you have the money in a short-term case, but what about in the long-term? What if, over the course of her life, they have 25 friends who are looking for the exact same product you offer? Guess who will be at the back of the list when they give their friend a recommendation?

You might be wondering where the PR aspect comes into this tip, and to that I say Damage Control. If/when you fuck up, and a customer is angry at you, and starts blogging about their horrible experience at your company, you're going to experience bad press. Refunding that person before they have a chance to destroy your reputation is an opportunity you should take every time.

Things rarely vanish from the internet - you'll have to deal with the repercussions of that negative Facebook post/tweet/bad review until you close up shop. By offering a refund, even if you think they're the last person in the world to deserve it, you will defuse a hostile situation that may warrant that person to otherwise go and complain about your business online to all of their friends.

Suck it up, swallow your pride, and just refund them.

Chapter 6: Sales

Selling is at the core of any business, and a business run by teen entrepreneurs are no different. Luckily for you, Howdy and I have spent over $75,000 on sales training programs, and we know what works and what doesn't for teen entrepreneurs.

"You can't climb the ladder of success with your hands in your pocket." - Arnold Schwarzenegger

"If you don't ask, the answer is always no" - Nora Roberts

"Cold calling is one of the most difficult parts of selling. An old sales cliche says that the hardest door for a salesman to open is the car door."
- Anonymous

The definition of sales is convincing somebody to do something - selling them. In the world of business, most often, it's focused on exchanging a product/service for cash, but selling can take many forms. Convincing your friends to choose a certain restaurant is a form of selling.

As I've rehashed so many times so far, the fact that you're a teenager will come with pros and cons when you're interacting with prospects, vendors, and third parties. This is one of the times where being a teen entrepreneur will help your case.

People love supporting teens that are doing great things. It's evolved into a cultural norm by now. When you see girl scouts selling cookies, you feel like an asshole if you don't buy a few boxes. It's important to use your status as a teen entrepreneur to your advantage.

If there was one rule that you had to follow every single time you engaged with a prospect, it should be "Never Stop Being Friendly". Being a jerk will never help you sell something.

Teens have a stereotype that's still in effect from the late 50s that we're all trouble makers.

And while that's still true for an alarmingly portion of kids, the vast majority of teens don't do anything wrong other than have the occasional drink or experiment with some drugs.

Your work will force you to interact with adults - Generation X and Baby Boomers.

These generations grew up with the stereotypical smoking, making out in the back of cars, etc. Their comprehension on teenagers, by default, isn't that high. That's why it's super important for you to never stop being friendly.

Just by being friendly and polite, you're already setting yourself apart in their mind.

Even if you somehow manage to scale your business without interacting with a single adult (and your target market is teenagers), being friendly, polite, and professional never hurt anybody. Your friends don't talk behind your back saying "They're just not enough of an asshole to warrant me buying from them.".

Making sure your interactions are appropriate and polite will cement great habits as you grow yourself, but will also protect you from the harsh world of offense and criticism.

You hear about things in the news all of the time - somebody loses an opportunity because of something they said, or somebody gets fired because of something racist they posted online. Don't be that person!

By staying in a default state of polite and friendly behavior, you'll never give anybody any leverage to make those claims against you.

Here's a nice exercise you can do. When you wake up in the morning, make it a habit to smile at the first 25 people you encounter in the day, and say "Hello!", "Good Morning!", or "You look nice!", etc. to the first 10. Just give this a try and see what happens! Your actions in the very first hours of the day set an example your brain can follow for the rest of the day without any conscious thought.

Always Agree

In addition to always being polite, it's important that you always agree with your prospect. Even if you're facing unrealistic and ridiculous objections, or the prospect is full-on yelling at you, mirroring that kind of attitude and behavior is a guarantee that you will NOT make a sale.

You need to deliver a great attitude by communicating positively at all times with your prospect (the person who you're looking to convince). This isn't a hard to understand concept -

a great attitude is a weapon. Point it at a person, and use it correctly, and it can be lethal in getting you the result you want.

Just like if you're polite, a lot of the adults in the world are now associating teens with being lazy, entitled kids who don't want to work. Even if you don't think this is true, (which I don't think it is), this is a tool you can use to your advantage. Entering a situation with a great attitude will set you apart as a teen entrepreneur. Pair it with being nice, kind, and polite, and you'll be unstoppable. A great attitude isn't just about standing in front of a mirror and saying nice things to yourself. Self-confidence is only part of it.

This is about you making sure that your head is in the right place. Communicating positively is a two-way action. There's no need to tell yourself how great your attitude is, because you're not the one you're trying to sell!

Every time you say no to the prospect, you shut down your chances more and more of getting them to hand you a credit card. Always agreeing with the prospect means turning "I can't" into "Can do!", even if you're not sure how you're going to get it done. You very rarely, if ever, say the word "no" to a person who's trying to give you money. If they want 250 items, and you only have 200, that's a swell problem to have. Commit first, and figure out the rest later. Use the cash they pay you with to get some more product in-house. If they say they need something done in four days, and you can only get it done in six, it doesn't matter! Say, "Of course we can do that! It will come with an extra rush fee that equals 25% of the purchase price", and take advantage of this new opportunity that you wouldn't have had if you had said no.

Phrases like: "Excellent!", "No problem!", "You got it!", and "I'd be happy to!" are all examples of agreeing with the buyer, and having a great attitude that will stay with the customer as you walk them through the sale. Your job, as a business, is to make money. Whatever they want, you need to move heaven and earth to get it for them, and charge them extra.

When you're dealing with objections, "The price is too high!", or "I'm not sure we need it.", you should still agree with the prospect. At first, this may seem a little bit out-of-balance, and for good reason. They're giving you a valid reason that they don't want to buy, and you're agreeing with them? What?

However, when you follow-up immediately with a rebuttal to their question/objection, something happens when you start off your sentence with "I completely understand, Thomas", or "Sally, I totally agree with you!".

The prospect's mind, in that split second, validates that praise just as you're going into your rebuttal. Even if they're dead wrong, agreeing with their frame of mind will only do you good. Nothing bad can happen with agreeing with your prospect. It makes it seem like you understand them personally - their wins, their losses, and what you, as a business owner, can do to help them. As a teen entrepreneur, your time is a valuable asset that will only grow to be more valuable as you scale your business.

Handling Inbound Calls

You want to keep the sales process, from the moment a prospect calls you, to the moment they hand you a check, as short and concise as possible. The more time you save per call, the more calls you can answer, and the more money you can make - it's common sense.

There's a specific way to answer inbound calls that will get to the center of what the prospect is looking for, and will let you know straight away how you can help. The incoming call is an opportunity where a potential customer is calling you to make an inquiry. We don't know if they're on the right product/service, we don't know their timelines, we don't even know if they can afford it! All we know is that they're interested, and they're calling for one reason: Information.

The only reason someone picks up the phone and calls a business is to get information that they either can't find online, or want to talk to someone about. These callers are also not interested in building rapport, or chatting about the weather - they're looking to get information and get out.

Don't bother answering the phone with something stupid like "It's a magical day at Tim's Landscaping, my name is Nathan, how can I serve you today?" They're not interested in any of that. Every word you say needs to be carefully plotted out so you don't piss off the prospect, but so you leave the door open to have them continue down the sales cycle. This caller is calling to determine whether its worth their while to pursue working with your business. If they're calling for information, cut right to the chase.

At Howdy Interactive, we open all of our calls with "Howdy Interactive, this Nathan, what can I get you information on?" It cuts right to the question in their mind. Believe me, your potential customers will thank you. It can certainly tip the scales in your favor. However, it will just tip the scales - you need to do the majority of the work. A big part of that is having a great first impression. First impressions matter. You were probably told that by the same person who told you not to judge a book by its cover, go figure.

First Impressions

When you're trying to sell somebody on your product or service, the first impression is the most important part of the process. It's the great equalizer - it shows who knows what they're doing and who doesn't. You have five seconds before the person you're trying to judge has finalized their opinion of you. If, for some reason, you had a bad start, you have about 10 seconds to try and make it work, or you're a complete lost cause - there's no way in hell they'll trust you.

Teen entrepreneurs are already at a disadvantage because of their age. Age directly signifies lack of experience in the world of business, something that we're trying to change. However, for now, you're stuck with the stereotype. The burden is on you to switch things around.

In the first five seconds, you need to show the person you're speaking with that you:

1. Know what you're talking about.
2. Are very passionate about what you're talking about.
3. Can help them solve a problem, and
4. Can help them do so in a way that they shouldn't waste their time talking to anyone else.

That's a big task, and it'll certainly take practice to nail your pitch down correctly. These four things must come across in the first five seconds of an interaction. Hopefully, with practice, you'll nail them every time, and then focus on re-affirming the prospect's mental decision that you know what you're talking about.

I can't tell you how important the opening is. I almost think it's more important than any other part of the sales cycle. If you can't convince them that you're an expert in your industry, you're sharp, you're passionate, and you want to help them, then you basically have no chance of walking them further down the sale. Think about it - would you prefer to do business with some bored schmuck from India cold-calling a general list about web design services? Or, would you prefer to work with somebody who immediately cuts to the chase about websites and it makes it sound like they know what they're talking about?

I'll give you a hint - 100 out of 100 people would choose to talk to the second guy.

Who do you think Peyton Manning or Tom Brady want training them leading up to Super Bowl Sunday? Some bloke from my local Planet Fitness who runs a side hustle doing fitness classes, or the best personal fitness trainer in the world, who's won Super Bowl after Super Bowl, and knows exactly what to work on for football stars?

I'm not saying that you need to become an expert before you start rolling in cash. You just need to look and sound like you do. Even if it's your first cold-call in a brand new industry you know nothing about, fake it until you make it. Establishing yourself with a good first impression certainly isn't the only part of a good sale - the sales process, depending on how complex your product is, may have several steps. However, if you screw up the opening and don't make a good first impression, you can kiss your chances goodbye of having that prospect hand over their money to you.

The Three Rebuttals

You'll notice, as you begin to talk with your customers and start pitching them on your product/service, no matter what they say and what objection they give, it always boils down to one of three objections. Take the price objection as an example - I'm sure you've said this before - "I'm not buying that - it's too expensive!". You might think that the objection does really have to do with price, but in reality, that's the last thing it has to do with. If the product/service you're selling them was providing the right amount of value for them, they would happily hand over what you're asking.

In the world of sales, there are three main objections.

- The person you're speaking to isn't the decision maker,
- they don't think your product/service will work, or
- they don't think they're going to use it.

They don't think it's valuable because of either objection two or three - they don't know if it works, or they don't know if they're going to use it. If they knew the product/service worked, and they knew they were going to use it, they would be able to approximate the value of it and easily be able to make that jump in their mind.

So what are you supposed to do? Your job, as a salesperson, is to treat the objection as a "request for further information". Don't get discouraged because somebody says that the price is too high, or they don't know if they need it. It's your job to convince them otherwise. Break down the barrier immediately.

Say something like "Sir/Ma'am, I know that's what you might think. But I've been at this a long time, and in my experience, people say "no" for one of three reasons. The first is that you're not the decision maker, which I don't think is true. The second is that you don't think it'll work, and the third is that you don't think you'll use it. Which one of those are we dealing with today, so I can be better prepared to assist you".

They'll appreciate your blunt honesty, and should happily give you more information on where their head is at in terms of objections. Take that and use the information they give you to your advantage.

Emotional & Logical Buying

Gerald Zaltman was responsible for largely pioneering the use of neuroscience inside of sales and business. I felt his insights on emotional selling were an important read for any teen entrepreneur.

An important thing to remember when selling anybody on anything is that we buy on emotion and justify our purchases with logic. However, according to Harvard Business School professor

Gerald Zaltman, we largely ignore this fact and continue to model our sales strategies to sell rationally - by explaining the facts and benefits of your product.

The main takeaway here is to incorporate emotional selling into your repertoire of sales skills. 95% of our purchase decision-making takes place subconsciously, on an emotional level, yet most of the world sells by explaining facts, figures, and benefits. Mastering selling on an emotional level will give you an edge in sales

As someone who's forced into a sales role to strive for financial freedom, we almost always default selling using rational strategies. Most people can't imagine, especially teen entrepreneurs (who might not have enough sales experience to know the difference), that buyers would ever made decisions based on emotion. Can you picture a Wall Street broker buying stocks based on emotion? You most likely can't, even though it happens every single day.

What makes our unconscious mind (where emotion is controlled) so amazing is that has worked throughout your childhood learning exactly what you like and don't like. It's the reason that you don't put your hand in a pot of boiling water, or you enjoy a certain kind of music more.

The unconscious mind has basically evolved to make minor decisions for you. Have you ever noticed you are walking to class, your mind is wandering, and all of the sudden you're at the door to your next class without actively thinking about the directions? That's basically what the unconscious mind is doing.

Sometimes, your unconscious mind can process small changes in your environment that either evoke good feelings or bad feelings. It's nothing that your conscious mind can actively detect (unless you know what you're looking for), but it's important none-the-less because it's why experts believe people can "trust their gut".

What your unconscious mind is doing is it's compiling all of these small changes and sending you a decision on what it feels you should do. The good news, is that this method can be taken advantage of. If you make small changes to the way you sell your product/service, it will impact the way your clients feel about you and your business. I spoke a little bit about psychology in the marketing section - how if you provide value upfront with education-based marketing, people will automatically want to give you something in return.

The same is true about sales. If you give something free away, like you bring your client a bottle of water on a hot day, or if you give away a version of your product/service, like a free room of carpet cleaning, your client will feel like they need to do something in return.

Steve Jobs was famous for this in his presentations - if you focus your sales discussion on how what you're selling can improve somebody's life, instead of the technical specs and logistics, people become more emotionally attached with the product. You provide those specs and logistics afterward (towards the end of the presentation) so it can be fresh in your client's mind when somebody inevitably asks them why they bought whatever you're selling.

Following Up

In sales, following-up is where the money's at - literally. I've known people who have harvested millions of dollars from their existing list of clients and leads they've fallen out of touch with. In sales, there's a popular saying that marketing is what gets the lead in the door, but sales is what happens after that - from the moment the client says hello to the time where they hand over their credit card. In a perfect world, that's how every single sale would happen. People who are interested would see your marketing, contact you to buy, and just pay you and get it over with.

However, clients vanish. A lot. They stop responding, they say they went with a competitor, they say they don't have the money, they say they don't have the time, etc. I've heard every single excuse in the book about why people don't want to hire me. And that's perfectly fine! I understand it might not be the right time. However, I'm leaving a lot of money on table if I don't continuously check if there's a right time.

45% of salespeople only communicate with their leads once, which is completely unacceptable. It's calculated that it takes an average of eight follow-up attempts to get back in touch with a lead after they've fallen out of touch. If there are really people that stop after one try, they're passing up a lot of money - don't make the same mistake.

Having a successful follow-up system is important for you to sell your products/services. You most likely don't need a full-blown CRM (customer relationship management system), which is business software that helps you keep track of your business contacts. Instead, you can just casually use the reminder app on your phone. If you speak with a customer and they don't respond to your email, just ask your phone to remind you in a week to try and get back in touch with them. If they don't respond, or they send their phone to voicemail, set your reminder for another week. Using the reminder app to keep track of who you need to contact is a great alternative for a CRM and can save you hundreds of dollars per month.

There are many ways to follow-up with a lead. You might just shoot them a quick email, or do something as elaborate as send them breakfast, a fruit basket, or a gift card to get their attention. The three best tools for follow-up are text, call, and email respectively. Furthermore, when you follow-up, it should be a dual event. I normally leave a voicemail and a text, or a voicemail and an email.

Keeping things non-salesy is a must for follow-up. I tend to keep things informal, using a technique called the 9 word email. Originally created by marketing mastermind Dean Jackson, the 9 word email is a non-confrontational way to revive leads that you haven't spoken with in a while. Just shoot them a quick message: "Tom, are you still looking for a house in Glendale? - Nate". The simplicity of this can't be overstated. It's not salesy, which compels the person receiving it to reading and responding to it faster.

There's a story I must tell whenever I bring up the 9 word email, about the best use of it - ever. A yacht company had a pile of dead leads that they had received from their web form online. A newly hired marketing intern, having heard of Dean and this method, started reaching out to these "dead" leads through email, just shooting them a quick message - no more than 10 words - asking if they still wanted a yacht. Because there's no sales letter, no pitching, and no hassle, dead prospects are more likely to respond. And one guy did. They took that guy through the (very short) sales cycle, where he ordered a $130M yacht, plus a $50M yacht to hold him over while his larger one was being constructed.

$180 million dollars of business earned with 10 seconds of work - just because they bothered following up.

Networking

Networking is very important. It allows you to get more involved with your local community and industry. The definition of networking is "interacting with others to further your professional relationships," - it gives you a good excuse to try and find people who are looking for your product in a social environment, like a mixer, or a conference. It's important to always be on the lookout for opportunities! Network with everyone who you think could benefit from your product/service - not just at these social events. I've listened to presentations at my old high school, went up to the presenter and got their business card. We had a few meetings after-the-fact, and they signed a contract with Howdy Interactive less than two months after the presentation at my school.

The local entrepreneurial community is very helpful in helping you start your business. I know I wouldn't have been able to do what I do without the support of my local community, and most often, it's where some of the biggest names in business got their start. Bill Gates and Steve Jobs didn't start by selling their hardware internationally - they started by selling to local computer shops. The same with RXBar - they started selling their energy bars to local CrossFit gyms. Anything and everything, from computers to food, can be sold in your local environment first before expanding.

Most entrepreneurial communities love to see new faces from the local high school/colleges, because they get to mentor and help you craft your life of business. They can help connect you to people who might need what you're selling, to vendors who can give you discount pricing, or to media outlets who might want to interview you. There's one guy I know in my local community - Joe Perry - who knows everyone and everything. I've been shopping at his business for years, and I use him as a resource liberally. There's no way I would have been able to scale to where I am without the help of my local community.

The easiest way to get involved with your entrepreneurial community is through your local Chamber of Commerce. Howdy's office are the two floors right above our local Chamber, we frequently meet each other on the way in/out of the building. Our local Chamber has members as young as 14, and membership to the Chamber of Commerce gives you access to a lot of networking events and contacts. It's important to start building your network as soon as possible - you don't want to wait until you're desperate for new clients. People can smell desperation from a mile away. If you just try to network to sell people on something, they obviously won't be interested in that.

Steven Aitchison says, "Life gives to the givers and takes from the takers," and it's important to keep that philosophy in mind as you're meeting new people. Try and keep relationships as win-win as possible! This will most likely mean that you should be referring people, introducing people, and having non-sales related conversations with people. The more you give to a community like that, the more you'll be able to take away from it at the end.

In the hustle and bustle of daily life, or while you're at a party or an event, you might find that there are too many people to talk to, all of whom want to talk to you later, want you to reach out, or want to do business with you. It's hard to keep track in your head. What I do is I open my "Notes" app on my phone, and after I'm done talking with each person, I jot down their name and what we talked about, as well as anything I need to do personally. Then, at the end of the night, I transfer it all into my CRM, but you can just set reminders or get those action steps done immediately.

Prospecting

However, sometimes before you have access to those types of networking opportunities, you need to go out and get clients on your own. That's how the majority of self-made companies start, and what's normally romanticized in the pursuit to financial freedom - commonly called "the grind", or "the hustle". Before you can just go to a networking event and get everyone's information who need marketing services, or their carpets cleaned, or a new phone system, you need to build up your network of clients and fans one-by-one. That's what prospecting can help you with.

Prospecting is the act of searching for new customers. Most often associated with cold calls, it's where you connect with individuals or businesses, one by one, and see if they're interested in buying what you're selling.

Prospecting has been consistently rated one of the hardest parts of the sales cycle, and can be brutal. I've known teen entrepreneurs who have spent hours a day reaching out to hundreds of people - firing off 300 emails a day, making 150 phone calls, and sending hundreds of texts. Those who continuously prospect and keep a full pipeline of people who want to buy their product are more likely to build that network where you can automate some of this. It's important to prospect even if you have buyers coming through the door, from marketing, networking, or otherwise, because one day, those buyers won't be there anymore. Without continual prospecting, you'll eventually run out of people to sell to. You can never run out of leads if you're chasing them down yourself.

When approaching prospecting, you're going to want to target people that fall into the same demographic you set in the marketing chapter - people who are impacted by the problem your business solves. Just like last chapter, if you're selling landscaping services in Maine, it doesn't help to start calling everyone in America when you can narrow that down. There are specialized tools that you can use to get people's contact information. At Howdy, we use Salesgenie and Linkedin, mainly. If you're selling to businesses, those are your best bets! If you're selling to consumers, just focus on Salesgenie. Both of those pieces of software have free options you can use to get started in prospecting, including filtering by state, city, income, and more. You can mold a list of people you can call by just defining your target demographic - it's like magic!

Finally, when you have a list of people to call, it's time to sit down and face your fears of selling to people. The only way you'll ever get good at sales is through practice. I've spent hundreds of hours on the phone just doing cold outreach, and I have a bit of a stutter! Repetition and practice help me work through it.

I'd like to share with you our award-winning prospecting strategy we use here at Howdy. It's called the 1-2-3 punch, and is modeled loosely off of Adrian Salamunovic's PR strategy. I always start by sending my prospect an email. It's short and sweet, similar in form to the nine word email. I always keep things nice and short because I don't want to waste time. My email usually starts like this:

Hi {First Name},

I'm contacting you because we're getting a lot of dental patients and we currently don't have a dental practice in your area to send them to.

Reply with a quick "Yes" with your best phone number if you can take on more patients. Reply with a quick "No" if you don't want to scale your dental practice right now.

Thanks,
Nathan

Sent from my iPhone

I used an example of a marketing company for dentists, but you can mold this to fit your product and service. At the beginning, it shows that you have an abundance of whatever they're looking for - in this case, it's dental patients. You then continue on by saying that you don't currently have a place in their area to send this solution to, which makes it sound exclusive. You ask for a small commitment - either yes with a phone number, or just the word "no", and finally, you wrap it up with an informal signature, and a casual "Sent from my iPhone" line that makes it sound like it was a spur-of-the-moment decision to contact you.

The second "punch" in the combo is a reach-out through social media. If you're selling something to a business, reach out through Linkedin or Twitter, as both are used in a professional environment more than Facebook or Instagram. However, if you're looking to reach a consumer, then you should aim for Facebook or Instagram. I normally reach out about an hour or so after I send the email, if there's no response, and just shoot them a quick note - "Hey Thomas, just shot you a quick email :)"

Finally, the third "punch" is a follow-up phone call. This places you in a position to control the call! When you ring them up, you can ask "Hey Thomas! Did you happen to get my email?" If they say yes, you now have a talking point! If they say no, you can walk them through their inbox, have them read it on the spot, and get their immediate feedback on your pitch.

Remember how I said in the follow-up section that it takes eight contacts to get in touch with someone who's fallen out of touch with you? Well, the same this is accurate for people who you've never contacted before - who you're calling out of the blue. Even if people say they're not interested (which is their natural position when someone tries to sell them on something), that's not necessarily true. People love to buy, they just don't love to be pressured to buy - remember the emotional v. logical section. It's your job to convince them that they actually do want to buy, and continuing to follow-up even after they've said no will help turn that tide.

Auto-Pilot Sales (For Service Businesses)

This is more geared towards teen entrepreneurs that are running service-based businesses - landscapers, cleaners, accountants, babysitters, etc. You might be perfectly content with running a service-based business, and that's great! However, on its own, a service-based business may not get you on the path to financial freedom as quickly as you'd like.

The path to financial freedom requires passive income, something that can't happen with service-based businesses. There's a ceiling to the amount of work I can do as just one person. Even if I was the best salesman in the world, I can only knock on 40 doors a night, not factoring in school, friends, extra curriculars, etc.

Last chapter, you learned how to auto-pilot your marketing. Now, let's learn how to auto-pilot your sales. Creating a physical product is the only way you can expand your service business after your schedule is 100% full, and you're making as much money. Creating a product will allow you to "auto-pilot" your sales by selling it online. You'll be able to, for the first time, create passive income for yourself outside of any investments you hold.

If building a product interests you, it's important to figure out exactly what kind of product you're going to create. There are plenty of options, but I can only help you with some of them. Here are some fantastic examples of products you can sell:

- A Course

A course is a do-it-yourself version of the services you provide. At Howdy Interactive, the average contract price for our corporate marketing services is $45,000. Not every small business can afford that - so we sell a cheaper course, the Kickstart Marketing Course, to smaller companies who can implement these tools and tricks themselves.

- Physical Products

With some chatting with manufacturers, upfront capital, and elbow grease, you can work on creating a physical product. If you're a local celebrity, maybe a bobblehead. If you're a landscaper, some landscaping shears engraved with your company logo.

- Membership Site

You can also establish yourself as the authority figure in your area by creating a membership site for your colleagues and industry professionals. If you're a landscaper, creating a group for landscapers in Maine and charging $9.99/mo admission would be a great way to get industry insight while reaping the profits.

If possible, you'll want to go digital for your product. Fulfilling a physical product is a pain in the ass, however cool it may look. For a little bit more information on why you should go digital v. physical, I want to tell you about Cole Schafer, one of my marketing icons. He's the founder of Honey Copy, and is on a quest to become one of the greatest creative writers of all time. If I may say so, he's well on his way.

Cole sells a copywriting guide (digital), and his book (physical), alongside his main business which is providing copywriting services to high-end clients. On the physical book, he has to pay for printing, postage, the tools to generate the shipping label, etc. However, on his copywriting guide, all he pays is a 3% fee taken by the payment provider.

If possible, focus on deploying a digital product, and advertise it in your day-to-day service work to your clients. See what happens!

Chapter 7: Hiring

If you've achieved a level of success where you deem it necessary to hire an employee or two, I'd like to congratulate you! You've reached a level of success that only about 3% of teen entrepreneurs get to.

"It doesn't make sense to hire smart people and tell them what to do; we hire smart people so they can tell us what to do."
- Steve Jobs

"Never compromise on hiring the best talent."
- Bhavin Turakhia

"Oh, you want an easy life? I hear McDonalds is hiring." - Harvey Specter

Hiring someone is a big responsibility, especially as a teen. You need to know exactly what you're looking for in a potential hire. You're at a level of success that only about 4% of businesses owned by teen entrepreneurs get to.

You can't think about this as a small task - it's an investment of tens of thousands of dollars per year to hire someone part/full time, and even more money to train them, make sure they're on-task, and to provide them with the equipment required to do their job.

So what's my real advice when it comes to hiring?

Don't.

When Jack Welch, the former CEO of General Electric, decided to fire someone, he specifically didn't hire a replacement immediately.

He wanted to see how long the company could do without that person. If they got on fine, he didn't replace them.

However, if their position really was that valuable, there would be a negative effect on the productivity of that department. In other words, they'd hurt. You can use this same methodology to approach scaling your hiring.

Teen entrepreneurs, myself included, normally have a grand idea when they taste that first bit of success.

They imagine hundreds of employees, working in a great big office with their name on it. I very quickly snapped out of that mindset because I realized it jeopardized my plan of financial freedom.

Why waste money on three developers when you only need one? I'd rather spend the $100,000/yr I would have used to hire them to travel the world when I retire.

We have a network of 170 employees, contractors, and freelancers at Howdy Interactive. However, our internal team, the one out of our office in Bangor, is just five people.

That's it.

We keep it small and agile, because that's all we need to do our jobs well. Our last hire was in September 2018, and we're thriving with five essential people. We're not hurting, so there's no sense in dropping $50,000/yr to hire someone who we have no need for.

If you are bringing someone on to join your team, make sure you know exactly what pain they are working to minimize. Otherwise, don't bother.

Hire An Assistant First

When Tony Robbins was a teenager and just starting his enterprise, he was running around and completely off-balance because of the sheer amount of work he was doing on a daily basis.

Not the fun stuff either - he was picking up his suits from the dry cleaners, he was waiting in lines, etc. Very quickly, and at a very young age, he decided to make the jump and hire an assistant.

He didn't start with a lot of hours at first - he hired somebody for just two hours per day. As his company grew, that two hours slowly evolved into four hours. And then a full work day. Then he got two assistants. And so on and so forth.

When you reach a certain level of success as a teen entrepreneur, there just isn't enough time in the day for you to do everything.

You can't do the administrative work for your business, and focus on school, and focus on friendships & relationships, and focus on family. It's just not realistic.

Even if you've crushed everything down to a point where you can do it all, why should you?

That time you spend doing your company books, or running to the post office, or booking travel would be better spent doing what you're good at - the strengths and traits that make you the best person to own that company. Whether it's calling prospects, or thinking about the big picture, or planning an event, focus on that.

Don't focus on the administrative work that can be pawned off to somebody else.

If you're still on the fence about hiring someone, there are plenty of services that you can use to outsource work.

There are plenty of sites, like Upwork and Zirtual, that you can use to hire a virtual assistant who can work for you a few hours a month dependent on what you need done.

Theoretically, you could also outsource your school work, but I advise you to go down that path at your own peril, and keep in mind your school's academic integrity policy.

When you outsource work, either to a virtual assistant, or to somebody who works alongside you part/full time, then you free up the time you need to take advantage of your own abilities and strengths, passions and dreams.

Unless it costs you more per hour to outsource than it does to do it yourself, or you enjoy doing it and it's part of your relaxing process, then you should outsource any administrative task you can.

Don't Just Hire Locally

My non-profit, the Maine Student Film Festival, receives about 2,500 submissions per year.

My team goes through every single one to verify that they are up to festival code, and it's a routine conversation inside of our business about how diverse the films are.

I finally decided to check a statistic, and exported all of the submission data for this year's festival. I loaded it into a data counter, and discovered a shocking fact.

We routinely advertise MSFF as one of the best collections of student films from around the world, and we're not lying. The talent of the student filmmakers is unparalleled, and we collect thousands of submissions and see hundreds of hours of amazing work.

Of these 2,500 submissions, how many do you think were from Hollywood, CA? The fabled, sacred land of the invention of moviemaking?

Two films. Neither made the cut into the next round of judging.

As a fun experiment, I pulled the info some films that did advance to the next round of judging, films that outclassed the projects we displayed last year. Here's a selection of a few of the cities that had filmmakers who advanced to the next round of judging:

- Tulsa, Oklahoma
- Greensboro, North Carolina
- Anchorage, Alaska
- Chesapeake, Virginia
- Henderson, Nevada

Do you notice something strange? None of those locations are anywhere near a film industry hotspot! And yet they still managed to make amazing films anyway!

As you look for someone to hire, your search may drift to people outside of your city, and eventually, outside of your state. I say this because mine quickly did. I realized that my second hire, after an assistant, couldn't be fulfilled in Bangor, ME. I would have to look elsewhere to see if I could hire them remotely.

I very quickly found my guy, Shay, in Wales in the United Kingdom. Wales, by any means, is not a tech hotspot. It is comparable to San Antonio, TX - there are developers there, they're very talented, but no large companies are fighting for employees out of San Antonio. However, for my needs, Shay worked perfectly, and has worked alongside me for over a year and a half.

As a teen entrepreneur who is tasked with hiring someone, the same teen entrepreneur who sees the light at the end of the tunnel of financial freedom, it's easy to center your search for remote talent in a talent hub.

However, doing so is a losing game. The average developer salary in San Francisco is $114,000/yr, while the average developer salary in San Antonio is $47,600/yr. See what I'm talking about?

The skill set between the developer in San Francisco and San Antonio isn't too different, but you'll pay less than 50% what you would have paid in a talent hub, versus if you had looked in places you didn't think had talented people like that.

Work Remotely

At Howdy, we have a little bit of a unique take on offices, productivity, and working. While we have our amazing building at 2 Hammond Street in downtown Bangor, it is a requirement at Howdy that you work from elsewhere at least two days a week, and more if you'd like. We have people on staff who've never stepped foot in our office.

Believe it or not, we do this so people are more productive. To illustrate this point, it's probably best proportionalized into an analogy that all teen entrepreneurs can understand: school.

Where do you go when you really need to get an assignment done? A year ago, I asked this to ten of my classmates. Some said their house, some said a coffee shop, and some said they like working outside. Notice what none of them said - their school building.

The traditional academic environment represents what Jason Fried, founder of Basecamp.com, affectionately calls an "interruption factory".

You get there at 7:30, are stuffed into class after class, with a few study halls and lunch periods scattered here and there. You're kicked out at 2:00, unless you're staying for an extra curricular, and then you go home.

Where are you supposed to get meaningful work done? The same dilemma lies within the workspace. A really busy place of business is opening you up to interruption after interruption.

Someone is asking for help, you're needed on a sales call, you're pulled into lunch with a friend, or you're somehow responsible for the office running out of pens.

If, as a teen entrepreneur, you are fortunate enough to get to a place where you're looking into leasing office space, don't make people work out of there every single day.

What ends up happening is in the morning, you walk into the office with things to do. However, you're very quickly pulled into a sea of interruptions, and before you know it, you've run out of time to do what you needed to get done that day.

Creative work, meaningful work - work that makes a difference - needs to be done in a long stretch of time where you are focusing on the work itself, and not the distractions that come with running a business.

The same goes for your employees. If you want them to get quality work done, don't make them work in an environment prone to stress.

If your immediate concern is, "How do I know if they're getting work done?", you obviously don't unless you install some weird software to track their every move. But you shouldn't. Unless there's a specific issue, an employer/employee relationship requires some amount of trust.

If you're not getting the work that they're doing, that's obviously another story, but trust your team - they want what's best for you.

Hire The Better Salesman

If at any point you find yourself trying to decide between a few people to fill a position at your company, always go for the better salesperson.

It doesn't matter if the position you're hiring for is a marketer, administrative assistant, programmer, retail associate, or whatever, but the sales skills will sell off.

By nature, their writing and communication will be more persuasive and will position you to get a better chance of what you want, whether that be new clients, or a new opportunity that your employee is trying to get for you.

Being a good salesperson is more about reading things off a script. Good salespeople know how to communicate, to present their ideas clearly, and to persuade groups of people to choose the right idea, all of which are important values to your success.

The next time you're stuck, just pick the person who sold you better on getting the job. It'll be worth it in the long run.

Chapter 8: Trial Week

I frequently get asked about what a week in the life of a teen entrepreneur looks like. The truth is, it varies greatly.

There isn't a typical week in my life, but looking at my calendar, a week in August 2019 was the closest representation I could find.

MONDAY

4:00am - I wake up a bit earlier than normal to hop on a call with Matej Pecan in Croatia! Matej runs the largest GiG development course in the world. Because of my experience in the world of game development, we're exploring the idea of me hosting a course under his platform. The call goes well, and we set a meeting for a few weeks ahead.

7:00am - I eat breakfast and get ready for the day. I almost never eat normal breakfast food, rather food that will help me function in the morning. Today, breakfast is tortellini with a creamy pesto sauce. I make it all from scratch - cooking helps me relax.

8:00am - I get pulled into a meeting with my legal counsel, Louis Snyman. We've received a pretty nasty legal threat from a local health & fitness company about some content on our website. We draft a response and send it off. Louis has been with me from almost the very beginning, and already knows what I want to say before I say it. He's a great asset to have.

9:30am - I usually spend the mornings working on creative projects, and today is no exception. I get started working on a home page design for a debt collection software we're working on under the Howdy Interactive umbrella. When I'm working on something like that, I'm "wired in", and nobody can disturb me or it breaks my flow.

11:00am - If school was in session, I'd be on my way to UTC, where I take college classes. However, since it doesn't begin for another three weeks, I continue to focus on the debt collection software. I order some lunch during a quick break.

12:00pm - My lunch arrives! I break and eat. I usually get lunch delivered, but I'm slowing down that practice - it's starting to make me very fat.

12:30pm - Dimitris, our project lead on one of our game projects, sucks me into a meeting to discuss an event we're going to in Athens for user feedback. We finalize a budget and begin the process of purchasing the branding items.

1:00pm - I supervise the installation of new studio lighting at our office at 2 Hammond Street. We're ordered them as a part of a larger plan to build a set for our content - our monthly marketing trainings, and our Kickstart Marketing Course. We pay a lot of attention to the way we present ourselves to our clients, and installing the studio lighting is a big jump in the professionalism of our broadcasts and content.

2:00pm - I immerse myself in administrative tasks - mostly paying bills and sales calls for the rest of the day.

My days on Monday end at 3:30pm so I have time to run to the gym and meet one of my music instructors, Tamara. I am on call 24/7 in case our clients need assistance, but the rest of the day is largely mine, where I get to eat dinner, watch Netflix, and be with family.

TUESDAY

4:30am - I wake up and get ready for the day. I'm actually feeling like eating breakfast food today, which is a very rare occurrence. My breakfast consists of eggs, sunny-side-up, buttered toast, and mango nectar imported from Moscow.

6:00am - I start my day by responding to all of the emails that have piled up throughout the night. There's nothing really important, save for an update from Louis on the cease-and-desist, so I pick up a book.

7:00am - I try to read as much as I possibly can, usually wrapping up about two books a week. I scroll through the front page of Reddit, and turn my attention back to my book of choice - The Way

Of The Wolf by Jordan Belfort, also known as The Wolf of Wall Street. It's a fantastic read, and I immediately start finding some ideas that I can implement at Howdy Interactive to help boost our sales.

8:30am - I'm sent an update on a web design project that we're working on by one of my web designers, Shay Punter. I annotate the files and send them back for revisions.

9:00am - I start the workday calling Dan Tremble, who co-owns a national chain of restaurants called Ground Round. He was a referral client by one of my dear friends, State Representative Joe Perry, who I've known for almost a decade. We're trying to get Dan on one of our marketing programs, so I give him a quick call and see if he needs help with anything. It turns out, we were a week too late - he called another company to help with some Facebook work the week before! You can't win them all. I set a note for myself to follow-up heading into the new year.

10:00am - My creative work time begins! I dedicate the next two hours to continuing work on the debt collection software project I started on Monday. I got so much done yesterday that I want to keep up the good work. At the end of my time being wired in, I send it off to the person responsible for the project for their feedback.

12:00pm - I eat lunch! This time, I try for something in the realm of healthy food and get a grilled chicken sandwich from Chick-Fil-A. I spend about 30 minutes on lunch, browsing Reddit and eating my food.

12:30pm - I take a nap. Benefit of being your own boss!

2:00pm - I dial into a conference call with Alex Grant and Joe Munizaga from Grant Cardone's office. We're trying to negotiate to get our team on Grant's sales training software. I'm not convinced, but they send over a pretty sound proposal. I send it to Louis for review.

3:00pm - I email Jeff Peoples over at Window Book. Their software processes over 50% of all USPS mail, and they've been working on a new product for the better part of a year. I've been badgering Jeff over the course of development to award us with a contract to market their new product, and he's slowly starting to come around. Like clockwork, it takes Jeff less than five minutes to respond to my email - they're still beta testing. Bummer.

4:00pm - I pack my bags for my trip to New York City. I'm going on behalf of my non-profit organization, the Maine Student Film Festival, and a new service we're creating - a streaming service for student films, designed exclusively for academic institutions to analyze student creativity. I have meetings booked with NYU and the New York Film Institute.

5:00pm - My day is over! Time to be with the family, eat dinner, and get to sleep early. I have a plane to catch tomorrow, and will be spending the rest of the week in New York City.

WEDNESDAY

4:00am - I wake up at around the same time every day. It's the same routine - I make breakfast and get ready. Today, breakfast is pasta carbonara with truffle infused butter.

6:00am - My Uber arrives to take me to the airport. I scheduled it the night before so I wouldn't have to worry about it.

7:00am - I arrive at Bangor International Airport, and head through security. I see a book on the bookshelf of a store that I haven't read in ages - Inside The Magic Kingdom by Tom Connellan. It was published in 1997, and didn't really take off -

however, I still consider it one of the best business books I've ever read. I buy a copy and decide to read it on the plane.

10:00am - I arrive in New York City! As I leave Laguardia, I immediately notice some changes to how Uber handles the thousands of people who request rides from LGA every day. I take pictures of their setup, always on the lookout for cool ideas for our live events.

11:00am - The ride into the city takes about an hour from the airport. The Airbnb I'm staying at is in the Upper East Side. How I am still on Airbnb, and nobody's discovered I'm a minor, I have no idea.

12:00pm - I grab lunch at a pasta bar near my apartment. It's delicious, as most food in NYC is, and I leave a good review on TripAdvisor. I head to the subway and start making my way to SoHo.

1:00pm - I stop by Google's office to say hello to one of my friends in their marketing department. No name because Google is strict on unauthorized visitors, sorry! It's a 20 minute walk to my meeting with NYU, so we walk over together and stop for some ice cream on the way.

2:00pm - One of the reasons I'm in New York is for my meeting with NYU! I'm meeting with a few of their film & cinema faculty to tour our new product and get feedback. It goes very well - they love our new streaming service. It's good news, and I leave pumped up, inspired, and motivated.

3:00 - At a Shake Shack outside of NYU, I hop into a quick impromptu meeting with Louis. We're sending another rebuttal to the health & fitness company who tried to hit us with a cease and desist. I scan through the document, look for potential issues, but there are none. I clear it to be sent.

5:00pm - I grab dinner and go see a Broadway show! I've seen almost every musical and opera in New York City, but I love re-watching the classics. I catch an 8:00pm showing of The Phantom Of The Opera, and my day concludes. Or so I think.

11:00pm - I lock myself out of my apartment and wander around Manhattan until my landlord can let me back in at 7:00am the next day. This is a 100% true story.

THURSDAY

7:00am - I'm back in my apartments, and I haven't slept a wink. That doesn't matter because I have several meetings and things that require my urgent attention. I don't have time for a nap. I don't cook while I'm traveling. I groggily stumble around my neighborhood looking for something nice to eat for breakfast, and fail. I end up at Starbucks.

8:00am - I learn that MINECON Live is happening in Nashville, and call a friend at Microsoft to grab a pair of tickets. Minecraft is one of the most popular games alive, and a big part of what we do at Howdy Interactive has to do with game development - we want to honor the greats. I send Zach Burgess, who works on our game design team. It never hurts to have your team mingling with the developers on one of the world's most popular games.

9:30am - I dial into a call with the convention team at Marriott. We're trying to narrow down a venue for the Maine Student Film Festival annual event, and they've sent us a proposal with three acceptable venues in the Marriott portfolio. We haggle a bit over pricing and branding opportunities, and I don't leave the call convinced.

10:00am - I wander around New York City, ending up at 30 Rock. I grab an ice cream from Ben and Jerry's and explore the studio on a private tour. I see the sets where Jimmy Fallon, Seth Meyers, and Saturday Night Live tape their shows. It's fantastic to see the sets up close and personal.

12:00pm - I grab some lunch at The Bread Factory, which means I deviate from my route to the New York Film Institute by 38 minutes. However, The Bread Factory is worth it 100%. I eat there every time I'm in the city.

2:00pm - My meeting with the New York Film Institute begins. It's set up similarly to my last meeting with NYU, where I'm showing off our service to the faculty. The vast majority of them love it, and we begin licensing and sales discussions right at the table. That's how you know you've hit gold!

3:00pm - Pumped up from my success, I make several sales calls. The most successful is to David Michaels at 304 Stillwater Furniture, who requests some information on our marketing services, but admits he's only doing it out of courtesy. I understand - he says that they don't have any more marketing budget for the 2019 financial year, so I set a note to follow-up heading into the new year.

4:00pm - I head to a business networking event. As the youngest there, I'm bombarded with questions about teen entrepreneurship and other fun topics. I answer as many as I can, pass out some business cards, and enter everyone I met into my CRM so someone from my team can assess their needs for marketing services. Always be prospecting!

5:00pm - I've only been to the gym once this week, I need to get my game on. I gain access to a local gym under the guise of "trying it out". The guy behind the counter gladly grants me a free week of access so I can see if the gym works for me. Unfortunately, I'm going to have to decline his offer.

6:00pm - I grab dinner and head back to the apartment for an early night.

FRIDAY

7:00am - I wake up super late - today is a free day! This is the greatest part of being financially free and your own boss. You get to enjoy life and not concern yourself about jobs, school, or work for days at a time. I take a walk through Central Park and stop by a breakfast joint outside of Trump Tower.

10:00am - I stop by Fox News to speak with a reporter about the deceptive practices that software companies employ when customers sign up for free trials.

12:30pm - I make my way to an escape room, and meet one of my friends there. The game is based on a high-speed metro car that is racing down a track. You need to escape before it crashes and kills everyone in your party. We manage to get out with three minutes to spare!

3:00pm - I head back to my apartment to grab my bag and head to the airport. I fly out at 5:00pm, so I'm running a bit behind.

7:00pm - I'm back home in Bangor! It's been quite a week, so I head to bed and look forward for the weekend.

Chapter 9: Resources

This is the end of our time together! I hope my book brought you some good advice and tips in the world of business. Now that you have the tools and strategies to begin thinking about financial freedom, the only thing that's left is to get started.

This book was a blast to write, and it was amazing getting the opportunity to interview some of the world's most successful high school & college students for this piece.

I wanted to remind you that this book is interactive! I've prepared lots of resources and a special, secret chapter over in the Teen Entrepreneur Toolbox.

To get access, all you need to do is head over to **go.Nathan-Sykes.com/retire-before-college** and let me know where I'm sending your copy of the toolbox, free of charge! It might ask you for a verification code, which is just "teensuccess".

Good luck! You'll need it. The journey to financial freedom is a tough one, no doubt about it. However, when you hit the finish line, you'll be able to celebrate your success and enjoy the rest of your life without any worry for finances.

The teen entrepreneurs quoted, interviewed, and seen throughout this book are some of the best in the world at what they do. Pablo Picasso and Steve

Jobs both said, "Good Artists Copy; Great Artists Steal" - feel free to steal the methods from this book to pave your own way to success.

Whether you want to keep me updated on your wins, get help, or just say hi, don't hesitate to reach out! My email is ns@nathan-sykes.com - I welcome all of your feedback and will read every single message sent my way.

I'll see you at the top!

Acknowledgements

The following people had a positive impact on this book in some shape or form. They might have been interviewed, taught me something awesome, or just provided feedback.

- Joe Polish
- Alice Cooper
- Ishan Goel
- The Folks at UTC and MCA
- Connor Blakley
- Dino Dondiego
- Jesse Kay
- Joe Perry
- Dan Sullivan
- Grant Cardone
- Alina Morse
- Patricia Ortiz
- Mitch McCarthy, Jeff Sanders, Regina Kelley, and Karrie Richard
- Mike Koenigs

Special Thanks

A special thanks to Jim, Louis, Shay, and everyone who is, or has been, part of the team at Howdy Interactive. It's been a great 3 years so far.

Furthermore, a special thanks to all of my clients who have allowed me to gain the knowledge, network, and credibility to write this book. Thank you for trusting me with your money, your marketing, and your reputation.

Made in the USA
Columbia, SC
16 February 2020